Presented to

_____

By

_____

On the Occasion of

_____

Date

_____

TOTAL LOVE

DEVOTIONAL THOUGHTS ON GOD'S LOVE

FRANCES J. ROBERTS

BARBOUR
PUBLISHING

Published by Barbour Publishing, Inc., P.O. Box 719, Uhrichsville, Ohio 44683.

Our mission is to publish and distribute inspirational products offering exceptional value and biblical encouragement to the masses.

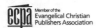
Member of the
Evangelical Christian
Publishers Association

Printed in the United States of America.

Contents

*B*eloved, let us love one another: for love is of God; and every one that loveth is born of God, and knoweth God. He that loveth not knoweth not God; for God is love. In this was manifested the love of God toward us, because that God sent his only begotten Son into the world, that we might live through him. Herein is love, not that we loved God, but that he loved us, and sent his Son to be the propitiation for our sins. Beloved, if God so loved us, we ought also to love one another. No man hath seen God at any time. If we love one another, God dwelleth in us, and his love is perfected in us.

Hereby know we that we dwell in him, and he in us, because he hath given us of his Spirit. And we have seen and do testify that the Father sent the Son to be the Saviour of the world. Whosoever shall confess that Jesus is the Son of God, God dwelleth in him, and he in God. And we have known and believed the love that God hath to us. God is love; and he that dwelleth in love dwelleth in God, and God in him.

1 JOHN 4:7–16

Total Love

Just keep on, My little one,
    And someday you will know
Why all the trials and the grief
    Were sent to try you so.
There never was a brighter day
    Than this you now can see,
There never was a sweeter song
    Than the one you sing to Me.
I've loved you through the darkness,
    And loved you in the light;
Whenever you have needed Me,
    I've always been in sight.

I never left you to yourself
    To battle all alone.
I've given you your sweetest joys
    When you My will have done.
I do not call you servant,
    I do not call you friend;
I call you My Beloved,
    And I'll love you to the end.
I'll love you when the way is hard,
    And when the night is long;
I'll give you strength, I'll give you hope,
    I'll sing to you a song.

I'll tell you that I love you,
    I'll tell you that I care,
I'll walk along beside you
    And all your burdens bear.
I'll give you hope and courage
    When your strength is almost gone.
We'll travel on together
    Till the day that we are one. . .
The day I call you yonder
    To heaven's open skies
When I'll gather you unto Myself
    And dry your tear-filled eyes.

I'll rid your heart of every pain
    And heal your every loss.
I'll give you joy and peace and life
    In place of every cross.
And what seems now an arduous way
    Will be forgotten there,
For in My presence all is new,
    And all is good and fair.
So lift your head and smile again,
    And let your heartaches go;
They only cause Me grief and pain,
    Because I love you so.
I love you with a tender love
    That is not changed by time,

And is not less for all thy sins,
   Nor could be more sublime
If thou an angel's form didst bear,
   Or thou a saint could be;
I love thee, not for what thou art,
   But what thou art to Me.
I see thee in the holy light
   Of My own deity;
I love thee with the *total love*
   Of all eternity!

*Our God and Father, in Jesus' name, we come to Thee with
empty hands and open hearts. We have nothing to bring Thee
other than our love and our gratitude. We praise Thee for every
divine grace bestowed upon us, and we praise Thee for Thyself
alone, apart from Thy gifts. In Thee our hearts find peace,
rest, and consolation. Thou art our source of strength, life, and
staying power. Thou art our joy. In a world of change, loss, and
decay, we are renewed daily by Thine indwelling Spirit, for
Thou art the unchanging One, and in Thee life is ever vibrant.
Save us from deadening monotony. Lift us above the sordid
scenes of the world about us, and let us be ever reminded that we
are "seated with Christ in the heavenlies," and let our spiritual
eyes view the beauties of the kingdom of heaven. Minister Thy
comforting touch to every needy soul, we pray, and speedily
bring to pass Thy will upon earth. Thine is the kingdom, the
power, and the glory forever. Amen.*

In Pursuit of His Person

Jesus knew He had come into this world to die. Beloved,
we also are here to die—to die to our sinful nature, our
unsanctified desires, our selfishness and willfulness, yes,
our rebellion and our resentments. We are here to die to
our right to ourselves, to our demands for satisfaction, to
self-pity, and to self-righteousness. In all our living, we
are forever dying, but we are dying in order to enhance
our living. For to truly live is Christ—to find life and live
life—is to find Christ and live Christ, and we truly live to

the degree that we are identified with Him.

We are ever in search of the clarity of vision that will bring Christ into focus in our personal awareness. We are in pursuit of His person in all the dimensions of His being. We are engaged in a quest to know Him as He is and to become more like Him; and the essence of Christlikeness comes not so much by our piety as by His purity. It is not what we are in ourselves so much as what we become in Him. We see ourselves grappling with giants of evil, but He is dispatching angels of light for our protection. We feel that we are trapped in time: He dwells in eternity, and He sees us in Himself—unfettered and unlimited. We need not grovel in the dust of defeat. The Overcomer lives within, and He is unrestricted by all physical limitations. Our liberation is to the degree of our conscious identification with Christ.

It is our love for Him that will draw us into union, and our love for Him is but the response to His love poured out on us. God is continually exercising the power of redemption. It is an ongoing process, working its way through every child of God—operating according to His will and ultimately bringing sons to glory. This is His mandate and His supreme desire. For this Christ gave His life. For this we, too, shall give our lives, until we can truly say, "I am crucified with Christ: nevertheless I live; yet not I, but Christ liveth in me: and the life which I now live in the flesh I live by the faith of the Son of God, who loved me, and gave himself for me" (Galatians 2:20).

Dear Lord and Savior, we bring to Thee hearts that hunger after Thy righteousness and spirits that long for Thy fellowship. Without Thee life is emptiness. Apart from Thy love there is no comfort. In Thy presence is fullness of joy. Let Thy goodness and mercy follow us all our days, and grant that we may dwell in Thy house forever. In Jesus' precious name, amen.

The Law of Patience

God is not to be bullied into bestowing His blessings. Once we seek His kingdom and His righteousness, that is to say, His rulership and His purity, we find we have in our possession the combination that opens the vaults of heaven's treasure houses. We seek Him, then, not in fleshly determination and stubborn willfulness, but in the unrelinquishing plea of the utterly destitute. It is the ultimate moment of "either-or"—the decisive crisis.

Every creative work of the Spirit of God within the human soul is preceded by devastation; for the Spirit moves as a whirlwind, wrenching out the offending thing, and then follows as a warm breeze on a quiet sea. For as the heart yields to the desire for Him, it finds that desire not satiated but intensified. The hunger grows deeper and stronger, for it can be satisfied only with His fullness.

But let patience have her perfect work, and accept patiently each growing pain as He enlarges thy heart; for His fullness cannot be received in a moment. Heaven's best is not attained in one wild bound. "We climb the steep ascent of heaven through patience, toil, and pain." The very hunger that seems to be a frustration is but His arm around us, drawing us ever closer. Chafe not at the reins, for the pulling of the bit is caused by the resistance of the flesh; for He knows the heart and tries the reins. His Spirit strives with our spirits until He gains the mastery.

Lay your heart open. Fear not the knife; for He removes only the proud flesh. He wounds only that He may heal. Doubt not His love nor His healing. He holds you upon the wheel until He has formed a receptacle that pleases Him for His own dwelling; and when He takes you at last from the wheel, He will fill you with Himself. Resist Him not, lest your vessel be marred in His hands. Chide Him not for His seeming delay; ask your own heart how many times you have hindered Him by your slowness to respond. Even now, by your impatience and attempt to hurry Him, you have become a hindrance.

"And ye shall seek me, and find me, when ye shall search for me with all your heart" (Jeremiah 29:13).

Our Father, we lift our eyes to Thee in adoration and worship, knowing that all our good comes from Thy hand, and from Thee we daily draw our life and strength. We rest our hearts in Thy love, like a baby bird in a nest. We need no other source of consolation. We ask nothing but the gift of grace to love Thee more perfectly and to understand how to share this love with others in such a way that both we and they may be drawn closer to Thee. Grant it, O Lord, we pray. In Jesus' name, amen.

The Eye of God

Reflections on Suffering and Afflictions

Daniel 6:20 reads, "Is thy God, whom thou servest continually, able to deliver thee from the lions?"

"Thy God!" Daniel's life had been an open witness to King Darius, the king of Babylon, who spoke these words. He recognized that Daniel was on close terms with his God, and it had been apparent by Daniel's way of life that he served Him continually. Ah, that was the secret! Daniel had not been serving King Darius, even though not to do so threatened his very existence. He served *His God* continually! What a testimony concerning a true witness, and it comes from the lips of a heathen monarch! It comes from the mouth of his would-be executioner.

Bless you, Daniel! In the least likely environment, you flourished in spiritual health, like a rose growing out of a rock. Yes, and the spiritual secret of this survival against odds is that the heart that is sold out to serving God is planted by Him in the rich soil of His love and is nourished by devotion. It is not dependent on any help from the outside. It is sustained by the inner strength of the union of spirit with Spirit. It will survive the cold of persecution and the flames of hate. It will come out of every experience unscathed. There will be no bitterness, no blight.

To rest content in the providence of God is to arm the soul with its most powerful defense. To dwell in God is to be engulfed in His presence as an image is captured in the eye. The worshiping soul is captured by the eye of God and held in His embrace. Daniel was not so much in the lion's den as he was in the *eye* of *God*. His love for God put him there, and God's response brought the angel to close the mouths of the lions that they gave him no harm. Devotion to God will bring the powers of heaven to the rescue of the suffering saint and shut the jaws of the devourer.

Suffering in the lives of God's children is a problem probing the mysteries of this life and the next. Some say we would not suffer except for our sin and rebellion. Sometimes this may be true, but it is not always so. Daniel was in the lion's den not because of his sins but because of his righteousness. "Many are the afflictions of the righteous: but the LORD delivereth him out of them all" (Psalm 34:19). How and when that deliverance comes is a matter partly of divine sovereignty. In the meantime, the trusting soul will rest in His love.

Life is brutal at times, but it is not the reflection of God's character nor any indication that He is unaware or uncaring. His love for us stands totally apart from our circumstances. It is in finding the reality of His love towering above our pain that we can be lifted from it even while we may still be in it. If I demand God to take away my pain in order to prove to me His love, I am on the wrong track. My pain has nothing to do with His love. He does not love the person who is well and happy more than He loves the one who is sick and destitute. He loves because He is love, and nothing changes His character. We have to separate our hurts from His heart.

Our hope lies in living in the Spirit—God's presence—where there is abundant life, perfect health, love, peace, and joy. When we get into that place and *dwell* there, and train our sights on all that God is—all His mercy, His forgiveness, His power, His majesty, His authority over darkness, His unbounded grace, and His fathomless love—the *goodness* that is in God will make its way into our consciousness, and as it does, it will begin to *transform* our darkness into light, our sorrow into joy, our desolation into hope, and our bitterness into love. His healing power will begin to manifest itself. The bitter waters will be sweetened, and praise will replace complaint. God is not hiding Himself in our times of desperation. Every promise He ever made is true. Everything He ever claimed to be, He is. It is we who nullify His divine love and power by distrusting His intentions when we need to be embracing His person and judging Him by how great He is rather than by the size of our personal pain. God is not in our pain. God is in God, and in God there is no pain, and we can get into God and find our strength and comfort there.

When we cease moaning, we will hear the singing of the birds. When we look up rather than down, we will see that the sun is shining. When we love and serve Him with the constancy of Daniel, yes, He will deliver us from the lions and from the pit.

And if healing never comes to us or to a loved one, should we complain if in infinite love and wisdom He gathers us into His bosom where healing is not only complete but eternal? Could it be disappointment to enter into glory and be released from the prison house of this body of clay? Is it defeat to be promoted and receive an eternal reward? No. For "if our earthly house of this tabernacle were dissolved, we have a building of God, an house not made with hands, eternal in the heavens" (2 Corinthians 5:1). Nowhere in God's Word are we promised immunity from the trials and tribulations of this life. No saint in the Bible escaped trouble, nor were the vicissitudes they endured the result of lack of faith. We invite consternation and confusion, frustration and discouragement, resentment and despair if we portray faith as a magic weapon guaranteed to eliminate all the unwelcome experiences of life. It is in our struggles that God builds within us confidence in His integrity and the loyalty of love that can cry, "Though he slay me, yet will I trust in him" (Job 13:15).

The human spirit in us does not want to hear this message, but we dare not distort the truth of the divine Word to please man's rebellious spirit. The Spirit of Christ within our hearts is witness to the fact that we need not expect to escape suffering in this life. But in every pain there is a promise of grace, and in every battle with adversity, an opportunity to rise to a higher level of endurance. And who shall dare to dictate to the Almighty what our lot shall be? But we have His promise: "As thy days, so shall thy strength be" (Deuteronomy 33:25). Is this not enough? In the words of the songwriter, "It is the way the Master went; shall not His servants tread it still?"

We can turn back and submit to weakness and cowardice. We can deem the price too high and choose a way demanding less sacrifice and accept a popular message that erroneously promises total reprieve from pain as the reward of faith. But true Bible faith is confidence in God. It is not a blanket panacea for every problem. "Our God whom we serve is able to deliver us. . .and he will deliver us. . . . *But if not. . .*" (Daniel 3:17–18). *But if not*, we will not defect. *But if not*, we will love Him no less, and out of that love shall eventually come our deliverance!

Our loving heavenly Father, our hearts turn to Thee at the beginning of this day, first of all to bless Thy name and praise Thee for Thy continued faithfulness and mercy. Our hearts have no home but in Thee. Our souls cry out to Thee, for to whom else can we go? Thou art the one and only source of life. By Thee we are sustained. All that we have is from Thy hand. We offer it up to Thee, lest we take it unto ourselves and grasping destroy. For if all else were taken from us, had we only Thee, we would have all. Let us not be deceived by the transient things of the world, for they are of no lasting value, and all will perish with time. Thy Word shall endure after the world and all that is in it has passed away; so let us treasure it above all else and hide it in our hearts, for it will be our greatest source of strength in the day of adversity even as it is our greatest source of consolation at all times. Keep us from sloth, and grant us with each new day the resolution to go on, knowing that every action of the soul Godward draws from Thee a response of enabling grace. Comfort, dear Lord, the sick, the dying, and all who mourn. In Jesus' name, amen.

On Enduring Hardness

Endure hardness, as a good soldier of Jesus Christ" (2 Timothy 2:3). Enduring is a wonderful thing. James 5:11 says, "Behold, we count them happy which *endure*. Ye have heard of the patience of Job, and have seen the end of the Lord; that the Lord is very pitiful, and of tender mercy." Matthew 24:13 reads, "But he that shall *endure* unto the end, the same shall be saved." And it was written of Jesus in Hebrews 12:2–4, 7: "Who for the joy that was set before him *endured* the cross, despising the shame, and is set down at the right hand of the throne of God. For consider him that *endured* such contradiction of sinners against himself, lest ye be wearied and faint in your minds. Ye have not yet resisted unto blood, striving against sin. . . . If ye *endure* chastening, God dealeth with you as with sons; for what son is he whom the father chasteneth not?"

Indeed, so much is said about endurance in the Word of God that we would be greatly advantaged to give it more consideration. Not all unfavorable circumstances in life can be changed by one quick miracle or one simple prayer, however great our faith. The famous "alcoholic's prayer" has considerable merit and wisdom: "God, grant me the serenity to accept the things I cannot change, courage to change the things I can, and wisdom to know the difference." There are many difficulties in life that yield to believing power and faith. There are others that greet us every morning despite the most fervent supplication for their removal. These are the things that call for endurance. If this is an unacceptable thought, then at least we must surely agree that *until* they shall be changed or removed from our lives, we do well to preserve our peace and equanimity of spirit by "enduring the hardness as good soldiers." Hebrews 6:15 says of Abraham that "after he had patiently *endured*, he obtained the promise." And of Moses the Bible says, "By faith he forsook Egypt, not fearing the wrath of the king: for he *endured*, as seeing him who is invisible" (Hebrews 11:27).

We have by no means exhausted the scriptures on this subject, but the foregoing should be sufficient to point out the fact that faith and prayer have a counterpart in patience and endurance. Ephesians 6:13 reads, "Wherefore take unto you the whole armour of God, that ye may be able to withstand in the evil day, *and having done all*, to *stand*." Having done all what? Having prayed and believed and committed and released the problem to God, if it still persists, then stand—*endure*—wait in patience, and faint not. Jesus said, "Blessed is he, whosoever shall not be offended in me" (Matthew 11:6). Blessed are those who are not in consternation when things seem to be going wrong. Blessed are those who do not pout when answers to prayer are delayed. Blessed are those who can and do keep on praising when the battle seems to be going against them. *God is still on the throne.* Victory is secured. Right does triumph over wrong. Evil will be avenged. Morning does come, however long and black the night. "Behind a frowning providence God hides a smiling face."

I was never more acutely aware of the loving care and protection of my mother and father than the night we arrived in Florida when the sky was churning with black clouds of an approaching hurricane. The house we expected to rent was occupied, and we were directed to an empty house in the middle of a palmetto field. When we were put to bed, my mother simply said we could sleep in our clothes. I was eight years old, but I realized she was thinking that we might have to get out of the house before morning.

Storms can be very frightening, but the grace of God

is always given in proportionate measure to the exigency, and never is He more precious than in the moments of dire human distress. How beautiful His loving touch in the hour of great need. How reassuring His voice in the midst of the storm. Don't I believe in faith and miracles? Yes, of course I do. The Bible and human history are full of faith and miracles. Testimonies abound in healings and deliverances from all manner of sicknesses and bondages. Praise God! He is in the business of miracles. He is the same yesterday, today, and forever. He is on our side. He is the One who parted the Red Sea, healed the leper, opened blind eyes, raised the dead, and is still doing mighty wonders in response to faith. But He is also the One who accepted and endured the cross with all its suffering and shame. It was the apostle Paul who wrote, "Unto you it is given in the behalf of Christ, not only to believe on him, but also to suffer for his sake" (Philippians 1:29).

O beloved, any half-truth is not truth; it is false. Every truth needs the balance of its counterpart. God is not out to pamper our "druthers." We would "druther" have instantaneous deliverance from an unpleasant situation than to be put upon to endure until. . . We would "druther" have a miracle healing than to suffer pain. What God will see that we have is what God sees that we *need*, not what we protest we *prefer*. When in trouble of any kind, a good prayer to pray is "Dear God, whatever I am to learn through this experience, let me learn it quickly so that I may the sooner be delivered," for rest assured, every circumstance in which we find ourselves has in it a lesson meant to teach us some valuable bit of wisdom or to strengthen our moral fiber.

Joseph never would have come into a place of power through which he could be used to save his people if he had lost his faith and allowed his spirit to degenerate through the long years spent in prison. If he had kept a diary of his thoughts in communion with God while in prison, we would be able to read the untold story of the making of a spiritual leader. Spiritual leaders don't pop up like a jack-in-the-box. Spiritual leaders are trained, like Moses, on the back side of the desert; like David out on the hillside; like John the Baptist in the wilderness; like Paul in Arabia; and like every man or woman who has been used by God in a mighty way.

Isolation, tribulation, persecution, and all manner of discipline are brought to bear upon the human soul to shape it and mold it to yield to the divine will. Why? Because we are all too ornery to be of any use to God or man any other way. *Jesus learned obedience through the things He suffered.* Do you think you or I will learn obedience any other way? Do you think God can produce "good soldiers" by catering to our every whim? Perhaps the real question is in the desire realm. Do we desire only that our every wish be granted and every need be fulfilled, or do we desire to bear the divine image at any cost? We sing it: "To be like Jesus, to be like Jesus, all I ask, to be like Him. . ." If that is truly our prayer, we can expect some pruning and chastening, for we have a long way to go before the similarity is conspicuous. We can compare ourselves to others who seem to be far less "spiritual" than we perceive ourselves to be, but the disparity between what we are and what Jesus is becomes increasingly glaring as we gain a fuller concept of the beauty and holiness of the Son of God. And that is truly the goal that is set before us: to grow in spiritual stature to conform to the likeness of Christ. The grace of God is extended to the believer for his perfection and sanctification. "Till we all come in the unity of the faith, and of the knowledge of the Son of God, unto a perfect man, unto the measure of the stature of the fulness of Christ" (Ephesians 4:13).

This is the desire of Christ for us: that we should grow into His likeness, which is to say, His character and personality. Let's not short-circuit the work of the Holy Spirit in our lives as He purposes to effect the perfection of our spiritual man. And how can we short-circuit His Spirit in our lives? By carnal desires and interests. Call it "faith and prosperity" if you wish. God calls it *carnality* and self-interest. If He has His way, He is more apt to give us what we *don't* want than what we want. If what we truly desire is to grow in grace and in the knowledge of Christ, He will move all heaven and earth if necessary to bring it to pass. The Bible says, "Seek first the kingdom of heaven, and all these things shall be added." We are not told to seek prosperity as an end in itself, but rather, to seek *Him*, who in turn will add the other blessings as He sees best.

Solomon was the richest man in the world, but he did not pray for riches, but for *wisdom*. We are reminded that "the fear of the Lord is the beginning of wisdom" (or wisdom begins with reverence and devotion to God). All self-seeking is a denial of Christ, and modern materialism is the spirit of antichrist. In the Old Testament it took the form of the worship of Baal. The world and all that is in it are perishing. The Word of God is eternal. The Spirit of God within us is nourished with heavenly manna. May God deliver us and protect our souls from hankerings after Egypt. We brought nothing into this world, and we will take nothing out. God clothes the lily, and He will clothe His children. He feeds the birds, and He will feed His children, but we do not need to develop great faith to increase worldly goods, but great grace to seek righteousness.

Love Knocks on the Door

We get out of sorts with God and with others when our selfish demands are not satisfied. We are seldom sufficiently objective to know or even consider whether or not those demands are reasonable, or whether the thing we are demanding is for our present or ultimate good. We can expect to be disappointed if we make irresponsible demands on God, and likewise, when we put demands on one another. God is not obligated to respond to self-serving demands that we place on Him, nor are we obligated to satisfy similar demands put on us by others.

Coercion has no place in a love relationship, and we are called to love God and love one another. Love does not demand its own rights, nor sulk when deprived some cherished wish. Love knows how to patiently wait for an answer, and can accept a no as gracefully as a yes. Love will knock on a door but will not force it open. Love is never disappointed when a desire is not granted, because it does not pursue its own good. It has subjected its own will to the will of the Father and has no selfish interests.

Loving heavenly Father, we come to Thee with grateful hearts, thanking Thee for every kindness bestowed, every danger averted, every burden lifted, and every obstacle surmounted. For whatever the challenges, Thou art there ahead of us preparing the way where there is no way and removing mountains that appear to be impassable. Praise Thy holy name! Thou hast not left us alone. Neither art Thou far from those we love and for whom we pray, and we thank Thee by faith for making the "all things" work together for them. We do not ask that there be no difficulties either for ourselves or for others, but through it all, we would sing above the storm, and hear Thy gentle voice assuring us of Thine eternal faithfulness, and we shall not fear. In the name of Jesus, we pray. Amen.

None of These Things Move Me

Whatever the vicissitudes of life, certain things remain constant. The Word of God is a sure foundation, the Spirit of God is our faithful companion, the love of God is unchanging, and the peace of God surpasses knowledge. Long ago the hymn writer penned the lines "Change and decay in all around I see; O Thou who changest not, abide with me." It is all right to pray thus, but better to *confirm* it; for we don't need to ask God for something He has already promised, and in this case He said, "I will never leave you nor forsake you."

To believe this and to experience it bring hope into the darkest day. There can be no sorrow without His consolation, no trial without His grace, no burden that cannot be cast upon Him, and no storm without His "Peace, be still." To rely on God at all times is to have a hidden source of strength far greater than all outer help. The outer help will manifest in response to the inner strength. The believer is not at the mercy of fickle fate. His destinies are shaped by his confidence in God—His Word and character.

It is somewhat frightening, but it is true, that to a large degree we ourselves, even sometimes by unconscious choices, bring about our own successes or defeats. " 'Tis the set of the sail, and not the gale, that determines the way we go." Happy is the man who sets his sail in the direction of the will of God, for he will find the wind of the Spirit driving him forward and carrying him swiftly toward his goal. Have you ever wondered why some people seem to move more smoothly through life than others? It may be that they have found the warm gulf stream of the love of God, and His divine energy is moving them along in the free flow of holy desire.

However that may be, of one thing we can be certain: He who embarks on the dubious course of self-will shall find the going exceedingly stormy, and he will be fortunate indeed if it does not end in shipwreck.

The mercy of God flows beneath the currents of His divine will. God has purposes above and beyond our own. His ways are above our ways, and His thoughts higher than ours. If we are ever to move in His will, we shall have to find a way to rise above the swirling forces of selfishness and carnal interests and seek the spiritual refinement that comes from concentrating our attention on the things that are above, where by His grace we are seated in the heavenly places with Christ.

Left to its own devices, the mind will occupy itself with matters at hand in this world of touch and see. Everything clamors for our attention while God waits patiently for us to desire Him enough to turn aside from this material world and seek Him in the solitude of devotion. Is it so much for Him to ask? Can we justify our persistent occupation with other things? Must He wait until the body is arrested by some illness or incapacity that will force us to give Him our attention?

Whatever activities we find ourselves engaged in, may our spirits be preserved in a state of peace and true joy by a sincere desire to make our love for Jesus central, so that whatever we do, it may be in the spirit of love, worship, and adoration for Jesus, the Christ, and our Lord and Savior. May we renew our dedication and serve Him with greater ardor than ever before.

Our loving heavenly Father, we come to Thee knowing full well our own frailties but trusting in Thy grace and mercy, pleading the shed blood of Jesus for the forgiveness of our sins, and resting in the finished work of redemption. For it is not by our own righteousness that we are saved, but by God's divine grace. We find our peace in the cross and our strength and victory by learning to dwell in the secret place and abide under the shadow of the Almighty. Bless abundantly we pray, all those who look to Thee for comfort and help. Let every hungry soul be nourished by Thy love; let the suffering feel Thy healing touch; and pour out your Spirit upon Thy people everywhere that they may be revived and refreshed, cleansed and purified, and made ready for our Lord's return. In Jesus' name, we pray. Amen.

The Kingdom of Heaven Is within You

People, places, and things are part of the human element in life. Too often in purporting to seek God's will, we are asking *where*, *who*, and *what* when we ought to be asking *how*. "This is the will of God, even your sanctification" (1 Thessalonians 4:3). God is desiring to have His will in our lives by working purity in our hearts, and He can achieve this under any outward circumstance. The outward influences are incidental. The deciding factor is the inward desire.

We ask: Does God want me *here* or *there*? Does He want me to relate to *this* person or *that* person? Does He want me to *have* this or *not to have* this—or that? And while we struggle for the answer to these questions, He is standing alongside saying softly and simply, "Give Me thy heart." That is all— but that is *everything*. We can do it in any circumstance. We can do it with a mate or without a mate; with a home or without a home; with a church or without a church; in America or in New Zealand.

God must be very weary of listening to our endless prayers concerning insignificant details by which we feign to be wanting to please Him while at the same time we overlook His primary and supreme command to *love Him with all our heart and strength and mind and soul*. Without this total love in our hearts for Him, we could go to the ends of the earth to preach the gospel and give our bodies to be burned, accomplishing only to waste our time and His. Conversely, if we really had this love fully operating in our hearts, we could sit still anywhere and bless the whole world. God is in no way limited. His love can never be limited. *We* are the limiting factor.

Freed to flow, His love is as broad as the ocean and as deep as the deepest sea. He wants not only to give it to us, but to teach us how to give it to everyone else. Everyone? Yes, everyone. Does He not tell us He makes His sun to shine on the just and the unjust? Did He not teach and heal and feed the thousands? Shall we presume to discriminate as to whom we will permit Him to bless? This was the point at which the religious leaders turned in blinding rage against the apostle Paul—when he made his announcement that he was going to take God's love to the despised Gentiles (Acts 22:21–22). Organized Christianity still picks and chooses, but God is looking for heralds with hearts ablaze with His fathomless, beautiful, unrestrained *love*.

Focus on Christ

My little children, how many times have I reminded you that I am to be the center of your worship? When your attention is on Me, you are melted together in a bond of love. You do not have to try to love each other. The love that you bring to Me rises like a tide and embraces the entire Body in a harmonious healing flow. It is so easy to direct your thoughts to Me, your loving Savior, and turn away from petty grievances. When My Holy Spirit is in control in your hearts, such things are swept away. The love of the Spirit, the peace of the Spirit, the joy of the Spirit are your safeguards against the warrings of your carnal natures.

Bitterness shuts out My blessing. An unforgiving, unloving spirit thwarts the move of God in your midst. Humble yourselves, and seek My forgiveness. I will forgive you as you forgive one another. Come back to the cross and to the cleansing blood. Remember again the price I paid for your redemption. I am more patient with you than you are with each other. I am more loving, more kind, and more understanding. I will teach you how to love when you have laid aside your pride and self-defense. I will lift you out of the pit when I hear your song of praise.

We come to Thee, Thou risen, living Savior, and we glory in Thy triumph over all the powers of darkness. We identify with Thee in Thy victory over sin, in Thy resurrection life, and in Thine eternal purposes. We look forward to the day Thou shalt fulfill Thy promise to come again in like manner as You went away. Speed the day, we pray, and prepare us in our spirits. Give us grace to occupy until You come. In Your holy name, we pray. Amen.

He Is Risen

He is risen from the dead; and, behold, he goeth before you into Galilee; there shall ye see him" (Matthew 28:7).

Our hope is renewed and our spirits are quickened by the beautiful message of the bodily resurrection of our Lord and Savior, Jesus Christ. The grave is open, the stone is rolled away; the napkin is folded and in a place by itself; the grave clothes are empty! He is not here; for He is risen as He promised, and behold, He goes before you. The text reads, "He goes before you into Galilee," but He would say to us today, "I go before you—wherever you are going." You may not know where you are going, but still He goes before you, and that being true, you may rest assured that even though the way be unknown to you, it will be prepared by Him. For yes, *He is alive!* He is alive and His presence is with us. This fact should produce within us a perpetual state of exhilaration. Our joy should be full and our feet light. Others have lived good lives and died; but only Jesus died *and rose again*, and He stands alone, unique in His power over death and the grave.

This speaks to our present need. This is more than history. It is a power-packed truth for today and for tomorrow. *Somebody* conquered death! *Somebody* escaped from the grave! *Somebody* broke the pattern and left the powers of darkness in dismay! Jesus could not be bound by death, for He was Himself the embodiment of resurrection life. He could break the chains of death like a ray of light can dispel a shaft of darkness. His unquenchable spirit of joy expelled Him from the realm of darkness and sorrow. Nothing could hold Him. The miracle was indeed not so much that He arose from the grave as it was that He could have experienced death in any degree whatsoever, even temporarily. To die was contrary to all that He is. To rise is His natural expression, for He is not only *life*, but the Creator of life. And we as believers are ourselves partakers of that life. We are united to Him by faith. We are joint heirs with Him in resurrection life and power. Knowing and believing this should catapult us out of our doldrums and lift us out of our depression. When Jesus died, I died with Him; and praise God, when He arose, I also rose with Him. "If ye then be risen with Christ, seek those things which are above, where Christ sitteth on the right hand of God. . . . For ye are dead, and your life is hid with Christ in God" (Colossians 3:1, 3). What a *dynamic* truth! What a tremendous reality! It should totally revolutionize every believer's character and personality.

We, too, may see death, as did Jesus, but it will not have a permanent hold, for we shall also one day experience resurrection power, shall break the bonds of death and rise triumphant over the grave. 1 Corinthians 15:22 says, "For as in Adam all die, even so in Christ shall all be made alive." Hallelujah! Lay hold on it, fellow saint. It is a bright star shining in the midnight sky. Whatever your burden, it will be less heavy if you keep your heart lighted by this glorious hope—this dynamic truth. And this is the gospel message: Christ died for our sins; He was buried, and He *rose again* the third day; He ascended into heaven, from whence He shall come again to receive us unto Himself that we may share His life throughout eternity. Praise His wonderful name! May the resurrection message never lose its bright luster, and may our eyes be ever watching for His soon return.

We praise Thee, our Father, for every blessing bestowed, for every challenge surmounted, and every victory won. We thank Thee for trials and testings, for joys and sorrows; for in every experience we are being disciplined in the art of contentment. Thou art the same, and in all the changing moods of our lives, the all-pervading strength in knowing we are ever surrounded and filled with the presence and power of Thy Spirit makes it possible to count it all joy. And so we look to the days before us with a spirit of rejoicing, knowing that at every point of need, Thou wilt be more than faithful to meet us with Thine infinite supply. Accept, we pray, our thanks for future blessings along with our gratitude for past mercies, and grant us an increase of faith that we may serve Thee more effectively and with deeper love. In Jesus' name, amen.

Well Done, Thou Good and Faithful

These words from Jesus' parable of the talents (Matthew 25:23) speak to us both in what they say and in what they do not say. What they say is "Well done, good and faithful servant." What they do *not* say (and we in this time and culture would be more apt to expect) is "Well done, *rich and successful master.*" We unfortunately have come to attach more significance to success than to faithfulness. Jesus placed the emphasis on *faithfulness*. While it is true that diligence is a vital element in achieving success, it is well worth our notice that Jesus, in commending *faithfulness*, placed emphasis on this character trait rather than on the end result.

The value to us in recognizing this is the encouragement factor. Many years of faithfulness may roll by before the reward is received. The final results are often slow in manifesting. It is in these waiting times that it is helpful to know that the eyes of God are watching our *faithfulness* and judging accordingly. Failure or success is not our concern at the present moment. The determination of such is in God's hands, and He will evaluate when the time comes. Meanwhile, our responsibility is to strive for *faithfulness*. In our own eyes and in the eyes of others, we may totally miss being "rich and successful masters." But it is quite within the realm of possibility that we can be "good and faithful servants." One of the determining factors, however, in our success in this is in truly making it our goal. The world, the flesh, and the devil have held before man the goal of the "rich, successful master" and have sold this kind of success image so effectively that it has become woven into our subconscious thinking that to be a "good and faithful *servant*" is little to be desired, if not actively to be *avoided*! We do not *want* to be faithful *servants*: We want to be successful *masters*. Herein lies our greatest handicap in following Jesus with pure hearts and sincere desires. It is written of Jesus that "he humbled himself, and became obedient unto death, even the death of the cross" (Philippians 2:8). Are we prepared for this kind of obedience—this type of faithfulness? Have we any true desire to be a servant? This is what is required of us. Jesus was a *servant*. He is called the Servant/Son. He was also Master, but His attitude as a Master was colored by His spirit of humility as a Servant.

There is an abundance of literature written on methods for achieving wealth and success. We all would welcome a direct route to the top. It is less glamorous to settle for surviving through the humdrum, but the largest part of life for most of us is spent in just keeping on, day after unexciting day, doing the thing that is at hand—meeting whatever challenge is there to be met—just being *faithful*. And the good part of it is that God is looking for nothing more than that—*faithfulness*; and to Him it is not a small thing but the crucial test.

It is easier for an athlete to win in an Olympic contest than for a weary saint to rise every morning consistently proclaiming, "I will bless the Lord at all times; His praise shall continually be in my mouth!" That is one expression of faithfulness. "To visit the fatherless and widows in their affliction and to keep oneself unspotted from the world" is another. Faithfulness is to be "instant in season and out of season"—teaching the Word. It is to be "praying without ceasing." It is "running the race with patience," "putting on the whole armor of God," "bearing one another's burdens," "looking unto Jesus, the author and finisher of our faith," "enduring hardness as good soldiers," "waiting patiently for the Lord," and "abiding in Christ."

Our cherished plans may not materialize; our dreams may not come true. Obstacles may seemingly block our path, and sorrows break our hearts. Can we in such times still hold our course and continue on to be good and faithful servants? This is what is required of us as followers of Christ. When our hopes are dashed in pieces and our dearest treasures snatched away, may the knowledge of

God's unfailing love sustain us in the darkness. James 5:10–11 says, "Take, my brethren, the prophets, who have spoken in the name of the Lord, for an example of suffering affliction, and of patience. Behold, we count them happy which endure. Ye have heard of the patience of Job, and have seen the end of the Lord; that the Lord is very pitiful, and of tender mercy."

The kind of constancy that causes us to continue to serve our Lord in the face of discouragement and difficulties is expressed in a lovely old Spanish hymn from the seventeenth century:

> *My God, I love Thee, not because I hope*
> *   For heaven thereby,*
> *Nor yet because who love Thee not*
> *   Are lost eternally.*
> *Thou, O my Jesus, Thou didst me*
> *   Upon the Cross embrace;*
> *For me didst bear the nails, and spear,*
> *   And manifold disgrace.*
>
> *And griefs and torments numberless,*
> *   And sweat of agony;*
> *Yea, death itself; and all for me*
> *   Who was Thine enemy.*
> *Then why, O Blessed Jesus Christ,*
> *   Should I not love Thee well?*
> *Not for the sake of winning heaven,*
> *   Nor of escaping hell.*

Not from the hope of gaining aught,
*   Not seeking a reward;*
But as Thyself has loved me,
*   O ever-loving Lord,*
So would I love Thee, dearest Lord,
*   And in Thy praise will sing;*
Solely because Thou art my God,
*   And my most loving King.*

If we need a motivating force to keep us moving in the path of a faithful servant of Christ, it is surely to be found in our love for Him and His great love for us. His earthly life set the example, but His love is the energizing power. His indwelling Holy Spirit draws our hearts heavenward in praise of God's great gift of eternal life through Jesus Christ, His Son; while at the same time His divine love poured out upon us seeks to flow out through us to embrace all for whom the Savior died. To be an open channel to express that love is to be a good and faithful servant. May it be our supreme joy as it is our greatest privilege and our most pressing responsibility. (See Ephesians 3:14–21.)

The path of dedication may run counter to personal wishes. It usually does. The divine intention is to accomplish the Father's will, not to pamper our selfish dispositions. Every new day is a fresh opportunity to lay down our own self-centeredness and be about our Father's business.

There are many times when we all have to pick ourselves up and go on; and it is wise not to waste time waiting for someone to come to our aid. There is an old Swedish proverb that says, "The best place to find a helping hand is at the end of your arm." That may not sound very spiritual, but it is sound advice. God is a very present help in time of need; He is a God of power and of miracles. But there are certain things He will not do for us. Maltbie Babcock's poem says it well:

> *Be strong!*
> *We are not here to play—to dream, to drift.*
> *We have hard work to do and loads to lift.*
> *Shun not the struggle—face it; 'tis God's gift.*
> *Be strong.*
> *It matters not how deep entrenched the wrong,*
> *How hard the battle goes, the day how long!*
> *Faint not—fight on! Tomorrow comes the song.*

It is true that there *are* battles for us to fight, and there *are* loads for us to lift, and there *are* duties and obligations for which we are responsible; and he who waits for God to do it all will wait in vain. Scripture says, "I being in the way, the LORD led me" (Genesis 24:27). It does not say "lying in a bed" or "sitting in a chair"! No! "Being in the way" suggests action and initiative. Our Lord said in Luke 12:50, "I have a baptism to be baptized with; and how am I straitened till it be accomplished!" Jesus had a mission to fulfill and allowed nothing to hinder. Beloved, we also have a divine commission for which we are responsible, and we should strive by His grace and in His strength to fulfill that for which we were called and chosen. Only as we do so can we hope to hear His words in that day spoken to us: "Well done, good and faithful servant."

It is a goal worth striving for. It is something worth sacrificing for. It is worth living for, and if need be, dying for; and it may require the kind of "dying" that is bit by bit, day by day, laying aside the pursuit of things that have not eternal substance or value in order to lay up spiritual riches in the heavenly kingdom. It may entail less conversation and more prayer; less sleep and more work; but it is a path of glory and a life of holy joy. Hallelujah!

*Heavenly Father, in Jesus' name, we bow in Thy presence to
wait upon Thee. We wait, not for Thee to do some special thing
for us, but for the quieting touch of Thy Spirit within our
hearts to silence all thoughts that are foreign to Thy love and all
feelings that would disturb the peace Thou givest. The world
presses in upon us, but we would press in to Thee, and to the
sacred atmosphere of worship. Grant the refreshing, reviving
power of Thy Holy Spirit to cleanse us from all unrighteousness
and transform us by Thy grace. Amen.*

And Jesus Beheld

And Jesus sat over against the treasury, and beheld"
(Mark 12:41). God is as interested today in the matter
of giving and receiving as He was at the time when Jesus
observed what was going on in the temple. But His deeper
concern both then and now relates to the heart attitude.
God is not particularly interested, it would seem, in wealth
nor lack of wealth, but He is very much concerned about all
that touches the spirit of a man, both good and evil—both
generosity and greed.

The apostle Paul says, "I have coveted no man's silver,
or gold, or apparel" (Acts 20:33). How startling, how
refreshing, and how utterly novel for an evangelist! Not
in the light of God's Word, but in contrast to the popular
trend, which is not new, but increasingly persistent. If
you had lived in Paul's day, you would have received no
desperate appeals for funds for him in your mailbox.

When we go on to read further, we find that he not only did not covet gold and silver, but says, "These hands have ministered unto my necessities, and to them that were with me. I have shewed you all things, how that so labouring ye ought to support the weak, and to remember the words of the Lord Jesus, how he said, It is more blessed to give than to receive" (Acts 20:34–35).

Can you imagine how much easier it would be to listen to a Bible teacher or a preacher who, like Paul, did not lay on you the burden of his financial needs, whether necessities or extravagances? Paul's desire not to be dependent on others but to carry his own load and share with the needy is quite different from what we see happening today. Certain practices gain popular acceptance, or are at least tolerated, not because they are right, but simply because they are widespread.

Jesus spent the greater part of His life on earth, not preaching or performing miracles, but *working* with His hands in the carpenter shop, making things and presumably selling them, to support the family in the absence of Joseph, who history tells us had died while Jesus was a young boy. And during the years of His ministry, He never got involved in fund-raising. The only time He passed the baskets, they were full, and He said, "Take something out," not "Put something in"!

Let those who wish to be successful in ministry learn a lesson from Jesus and from Paul. The first thing needed in ministry is not a mailing list for raising money, but a prayer list for intercession. Jesus came to minister to human needs. He was not concerned about how to get people to support

Him and meet His needs. He was about His Father's business, pouring out, not taking in. He admonished Peter, when sending him out, to *feed* His sheep, not to *shear* them.

We need, first of all, to examine our own hearts and motives; and it will never be amiss to also exercise some spiritual discernment in regard to those who practice coercion. We shall miss the greatest joy of life if we miss the joy of giving; but we shall miss God's best if we do not give as we are directed by the Holy Spirit, but rather give in response to the demands of others.

We read in the Old Testament about the "schools of the prophets." One wonders if our modern educational institutions for preachers may not be offering courses in the making of profits rather than prophets! One thing is certain: There is no lack of expertise among those of the cloth when it comes to raising money, and no end to the ingenuity applied in doing it. It is possible that the so-called prosperity message may be calculated to further facilitate the same ends, for it is difficult to have prosperity in the pulpit with poverty in the pews.

The most critical consideration is the fact that until the leadership learns and practices a spiritual principle, they of necessity deprive their followers of the teaching. Only a man who knows what it is to walk by faith can teach his people to do the same. And as long as the preacher begs from his people, his people will in turn beg from other people and feel no compunction in doing so. What is lost in the religious community through financial coercion is strength of character, personal integrity, proper sense of responsibility, and in many cases, even basic honesty.

Rejecting the "God is dead" philosophy, we act as though it were true when we see other people as our source rather than God. It is a beautiful thing to walk with God in the simplicity of trust. No power in heaven, earth, or hell can keep the blessings of heaven from being showered down upon the cheerful giver. When God's people are motivated by His love, their generosity cannot be restrained; and when their giving is directed by the Holy Ghost, it will be used of Him to bless the needy, not the greedy.

When Jesus watched those who gave, He was not so much concerned with *what* they gave as *how* they gave: not with the size of the gift, but with its source—whether it was from the heart. This is why He commended the widow who gave the two mites, not only because for her it represented a great sacrifice, but even more because in her giving, she gave in love as unto God, and not because she was asked to, but because of her own desire. A thousand dollars given to a religious organization in response to coercion is of no value in God's sight compared to the smallest gift given from the heart, joyfully, as unto Him. *Giving is an act of worship*, and for this very significant reason, when religious fund-raising operates on the mere human level of man to man and with selfish motives, it may very well be idolatry in the eyes of God. We may be sure of one thing: He is still watching! We are admonished that whatever we do, we should do all as unto Him.

Let us seek first the kingdom of God and His righteousness and trust Him for His faithful supply of our temporal needs. And let us "study to be quiet, and to do [our] own business, and to work with [our] own hands. . .that [we] may walk honestly toward them that are without, and that [we] may have lack of nothing" (1 Thessalonians 4:11–12). And let us heed the injunction "Give, and it shall be given unto you; good measure, pressed down, and shaken together, and running over, shall men give into your bosom. For with the same measure that ye mete withal it shall be measured to you again" (Luke 6:38). These are spiritual laws that operate in the area of finances. They work!

Honor Me

My children, heed My counsel. You have walked in rebellion and have followed the call of the world. The world and all that is in it are perishing, and those who seek after it shall also likewise perish. Seek life, not death, My children. Life shall be yours as you walk in the way of My commandments. My laws are given you for your preservation and for your happiness. I want you to be happy, to be free, and to experience the fullness of your creative expression. This can only come to pass as you refuse to honor your own self and truly begin to honor Me. You bring honor to Me as you fulfill My commandments. He who fails in being obedient to My commands shall heap upon Me grief even in his greatest moments of human accomplishment. You can give Me no sacrifice whatsoever but that which is offered up from a cleansed and submissive vessel. Then only do I draw joy and love and comfort from your devotion and dedication.

Heavenly Father, in the midst of the press of life, we pause to seek Thy face, to bow in submission, and to release into Thy hands every burden, every care, and every concern. Peace abides in Thy presence, and peace permeates our spirits as we learn ever increasingly to dwell in Thee. Thou art our strong tower of defense. Thou shalt be our advocate as we keep silence. Our love flows to Thee in an unending stream of worship. We praise Thee out of the abundance of Thy mercies bestowed upon us. Minister through us, we pray, to the brokenhearted, the afflicted, the lonely, and the oppressed. Make Your love known through word and deed as we seek to share with others the riches of Thy grace. In Jesus' name, and for Thy glory, we pray. Amen.

The Missing Brother

W hen I came to Troas to preach Christ's gospel, and a door was opened unto me of the Lord, I had no rest in my spirit, because I found not Titus my brother" (2 Corinthians 2:12–13).

Any concept of devotion to God that does not send us in search of our brother is minus an essential element.

In our text above, the apostle Paul comes to Troas to preach Christ's gospel, as the Lord had opened unto him a door. Reading on, it would seem that he made a premature departure, explaining that he had no rest in his spirit, because he found not Titus, his brother.

This is a poignant statement, coming from a man who is in so many instances displayed great courage and strength. We have here a fleeting glimpse of the tenderness of the apostle's heart. He recognized that God Himself had opened to him a door of opportunity to preach the good news of the gospel of Christ, yet his grief of spirit in not finding Titus was so distressing to him that he abruptly left for Macedonia.

This brief incident provides much food for thought. It brings into focus the fact that true religion is both vertical and horizontal, for we have a responsibility both to God and to our brother. James writes, "Pure religion and undefiled before God and the Father is this, To visit the fatherless and widows in their affliction, and to keep himself unspotted from the world" (James 1:27). It is, as expressed by Jesus in stating the first two and greatest commandments, to love the Lord thy God with all thy heart, all thy soul, all thy mind, and all thy strength, and *to love thy neighbor as thyself* (Mark 12:30–31). Romans 13:10 adds, "Love worketh no ill to his neighbour: therefore love is the fulfilling of the law."

In the words of an ancient Persian poet: "I sought my soul; my soul I could not see. I sought my God, but He eluded me. I sought my bother, and I found all three." There is a time to worship God, and there is a time to seek the brother. As we walk in obedience to the Spirit, we will find a balance in the two. It is the linking of devotion and service—of faith and works.

If we are sensitive to the direction of the Holy Spirit, we may find ourselves experiencing feelings similar to those of the apostle Paul at Troas. In the midst of the carrying out of duties, there comes a concern for a particular individual, and the sense of responsibility to that one person takes us away from whatever else we may be involved in.

This happened to Phillip when he was in the midst of a revival and he found himself suddenly transported by the Spirit to the desert to minister to the Ethiopian eunuch. We see the principle again in the case of Jesus being drawn to the Sychar well to converse with the Samaritan woman.

There are moments of destiny when one life touches another life at a special place at a special time with lasting effects. We should therefore never be so deeply involved in what we are doing, even if it be preaching the gospel, that we fail to be available to the Spirit if He chooses to use us somewhere else to minister to the need of some individual. For God is always concerned for the *individual*. It is our natural human instinct, born of pride, no doubt, to be impressed with the masses. Jesus preached to the multitudes on occasion, but more frequently we find Him touching individuals.

It is wonderful, when some soul is in special need, to be sensitive enough to hear the call of the Spirit and flexible enough to respond and go where (and when) needed. While it is not a literal transportation as in the case of Phillip, it is a very similar type of action. And to the one who is walking in the Spirit, these divine interruptions are as natural as if they were part of the planned schedule.

Our priorities and God's priorities do not always appear to be the same, but as we yield to the promptings of the Holy Spirit, we will more and more find ourselves in the place of His choosing, carrying out His will and purposes. The secret is in maintaining a flow of communication between the Holy Spirit and our spirit so that we catch the impulse. It may carry us next door or miles away, in person or by phone or letter. But it will always be fruitful, and beyond that, nothing will suffer in having been laid aside due to our obedience to His call.

And what of the times we are burdened for another but may not be able for one reason or another to write, call, or go? There is another avenue of outreach, often the most effective, and that is *prayer*. The briefest prayer of intercession on behalf of our brother in his time of need will be an instrument in God's hand to lift the weight on his soul, cover him with God's protecting mercy, combat an onslaught from the enemy, or ease his distress. The healing virtue of the Lord Jesus Christ flows from one member to another of His body, the church, by the unseen power of intercessory prayer. In answer to one of the first questions in the Bible: Yes, we are truly our brother's keeper. In our willingness to spend and be spent for one another, God's love is shed abroad, and through faith the powers of darkness are put beneath our feet.

Is there a "Titus" in your life? Is there a brother for whom your heart is grieved? Perhaps there are many, which would not be surprising, for the world is full of suffering and struggles. Let us be grateful for the awareness and commit ourselves to a prayerful response. There is not time for procrastination, and a selfish spirit will not make the sacrifice. Only love and obedience will keep us in a place where we can be touched by the feelings of the infirmities of others and used as a channel of blessing.

There is sustaining power that flows through prayer.

God has the ability to do everything Himself with no help from anyone, but He has chosen to allow His children to be channels of blessing. What a wonderful privilege! How we should treasure this gift and faithfully keep it in operation in our lives every day. Shall we not covenant together to spend more time at the throne of grace, both for ourselves and for one another, that we may guard against lukewarmness and indifference, selfishness and carelessness, yes, and sin and rebellion? There is no quicker and more effective way to generate joy and light in this dark world than by prayer, especially praise and intercession.

Someone visited a convalescent hospital and found one precious elderly soul in a wheelchair, her face aglow with a radiance born of an inner peace. When asked her secret of maintaining a happy spirit in such circumstances, she replied, "I decided, having found myself in this situation, with no possible way of escape, that I would spend my time here praying for all the other residents." Small wonder she was able to rise above the depressing surroundings and keep a happy face and contented heart. And if it works for her, it will work for all of us.

Our blessed heavenly Father, our hearts turn to Thee in love and adoration for all Thou art and for the many blessings Thou hast bestowed upon us. Though we are unworthy, Thy grace has been extended to us, and in Thy mercy Thou hast blotted out our transgressions. Accept, we pray, our love in return for Thine, and our gratitude for so great salvation. In Thy compassion be near to those who suffer, and comfort the sorrowing by Thy Holy Spirit who Himself is the Comforter. Send out Thy light to guide those who seek Thee into the path of life. This we pray, with thanksgiving, in Jesus' name. Amen.

The Tranquility of Worship

There is a way of the Spirit unknown to the natural mind. No barrier can keep you from finding His best except an unyielded will. As long as it is your inmost desire to know the will of God and do it, He Himself will guide and direct in all sorts of surprising ways.

His desire to bless you goes infinitely beyond your own personal desire to secure His blessings. There is always peace in His presence. Do not disturb this by anxiety to know what is in store for tomorrow. Out of the very tranquility of worship will be born the guidance you need.

Give Him your full adoration. His grace toward you extends through the channel of your love and is with the quiet knowing: Christ is in this day because Christ is in me. You can go nowhere without finding Him there, because wherever you go, you take Him with you, and He goes before and follows after!

Our heavenly Father, we come to Thee with grateful hearts
for Thy many gifts and for all the daily manifestations of Thy
loving care. We worship Thee, we love Thee, and we pray that
in some measure we may be given the grace and understanding
to express generosity to those around us and to all those
everywhere who in any way touch our lives. Deliver us from
fear of lack so that we may give with a free hand knowing that
in the stream of divine provision there is always a never-failing
supply of all things good. And in our giving, let forgiveness be
the crowning gift your children may all give to each other so
that brother to brother we may live in the freedom that is our
heritage in Christ, who taught us to pray, "Forgive us our debts
as we forgive one another." For Jesus' sake, we pray. Amen.

The Attitude of Gratitude

I once read a book bearing the title *An Attitude of Gratitude*, and I am borrowing it for this message. There is a touch of genius in certain catchphrases in that they have a way of lodging in our consciousness and coming to mind long after we think they have been forgotten. This is one of those, as it must be twenty years since I scanned the book, which is mostly gone from my memory except that the obvious theme was an emphasis of the importance of developing a grateful spirit, which at the same time is calculated to reduce grumbling and complaint. A happy frame of mind comes from a grateful spirit. A good way to start each day, before speaking to anyone else, is to say to your soul, "This is the day which the LORD hath made: we will rejoice and be glad in it" (Psalm 118:24).

It makes very little difference who we are or where we are: we are each important to our heavenly Father and each have a significant place in the kingdom of heaven. Our faithfulness to Him should have priority, and having established that, out relationship to one another will fall into place. "Let us consider one another to provoke unto love and to good works: . . .exhorting one another: and so much the more, as [we] see the day approaching" (Hebrews 10:24–25). The influence of one individual on another individual, and the total influence of all upon each other collectively, is a powerful force—for encouragement either toward total dedication or toward discouragement and desertion.

Included in the passage from Hebrews (mentioned above) are also the words so commonly quoted, often to the neglect of the accompanying thought: "not forsaking the assembling of ourselves together" (v. 25). The latter is more of an aside than it is the central point of emphasis. Beloved, it is very possible for believers to go to great lengths to emphasize the importance of gathering together and at the same time largely overlook the admonition given in the same breath to "consider one another," "provoke [stimulate, challenge, arouse] one another unto love and good works," and to do so increasingly more earnestly as we approach the coming of Christ. And for the sake of faithfulness to the text, it does not mention where the "assembling" is to take place. One wonders how much considering of one another and how much stimulation of one another in the direction of love and good works might be done between the saints if we were more aware of the simple fact that there is no reason to wait to do this until we are inside the walls of some specific edifice. The ancients have a saying: "In every conversation, let there be some words of divine wisdom." How much consideration do we give as to what kind of influence we are leaving behind as we converse daily (casually) with fellow Christians, and for that matter, with everyone with whom we come in contact for any reason whatsoever?

I have always enjoyed retelling the incident in the life of Alfred, Lord Tennyson, when as he was walking up the street with the morning paper tucked under his arm, a neighbor lady who was out in her garden called to him saying, "What's the news, Mr. Tennyson?" to which he promptly replied, "Good news! Christ died for our sins." Speaking somewhat loosely, for that moment they were "assembled together," and Tennyson took the opportunity to use it creatively to stimulate the faith of the friend.

The next time someone quips, "Have a good day," we might try replying, "Thank you. I am sure it will be, for every day is a good day with Jesus." It doesn't need to come off stilted or stuffy, but there are multitudinous ways in which we can share a word of faith or encouragement in honesty and sincerity, and with the same naturalness with which we speak of other things. It would be rather fun to make a special point to initiate our own little experiment in seeing just how frequently we may find opportunities to share our faith and hopefully lift another spirit by a word of wisdom spoken in sincerity. "A word fitly spoken is like apples of gold in pictures of silver" (Proverbs 25:11). What a beautiful way to express the potential riches awaiting those who share truly worthwhile, spiritually significant thoughts by way of everyday conversation. There is no need to wait for the testimony time in the worship service. Maybe the person who would be most in need of being aroused and challenged will never be in the worship service to hear the good word. Jesus was a frequent and regular attendant of the temple, but in no way did He restrict His influence to any one specific place or time.

Bless God for every church building, but, beloved, God's cathedral is the world! The Holy Spirit is longing to touch lives on Tuesday morning at the bank as truly as on Sunday morning in the chapel. It is wonderful to join the saints in worship in a congregation, but we should be equally stimulated to feel and express a true spirit of praise at all times and in every place. Didn't Jesus live like that? Didn't David write the lovely songs that we sing in church out on the mountainside tending sheep? We may limit ourselves, but you will never limit God to organized religion. He is everywhere, and if we will allow it, He will break through at every point along the way, and He will gently but surely let us know that there is some place in nearly everyone's heart that is crying out for His love. Be thankful; but do remember to *share* your blessings at every opportunity, and paint silver pictures with golden apples.

Heavenly Father, we bow our hearts in Thy presence, knowing full well our unworthiness, but casting ourselves upon Thy mercy. As Thou hast asked us to cast our cares and our grief upon Thee as well as our sins, we do so, remembering that Christ bore our sins, our sicknesses, and our sorrows Be near, we pray, to all who are experiencing deep trials and testings. Protect those in places of great danger. Lift the heavyhearted and grant peace and joy to those who carry burdens too great to be shared with even the dearest friend. Thou art our source of strength and help, and we rest ourselves and our loved ones in Thy loving care. Thou hast never failed to support us through even the severest storms, and Thou wilt not fail us now. We praise Thee from hearts overflowing with gratitude, through Jesus Christ our Savior, in whose name we pray. Amen.

Think It Not Strange

We read 1 Peter 4:12, "Beloved, think it not strange concerning the fiery trial which is to try you, as though some strange thing happened unto you." It is a settled fact that the fiery trial will come, and it is sent to try you, or by definition, to test, discipline, and prove. The admonition is that we should not be taken by surprise, not "think it strange," not be in consternation that such a thing would befall us. Don't be ashamed if you suffer as a Christian (v. 16)—do not think it to be a disgrace, but rather glorify God. Praise the Lord in the midst of sufferings and rejoice; and "let them that suffer according to the will of God commit the keeping of their souls to him in well doing, as unto a faithful Creator" (v. 19).

Granted, not all suffering is for the glory of God, and not all is according to His will. But the message running all through this first epistle of Peter is that fiery trials are coming to test our faith, and we are not to be taken unaware and caught unprepared in the Spirit. To quote an old adage: "To be forewarned is to be forearmed." We cope more gracefully with that which is anticipated.

What about Psalm 91, which promises divine protection and safety from harm for those who abide in the secret place of the Most High? Do we have a conflict here between the fiery trials of 1 Peter and the protection spoken of in Psalm 91? Is God capricious? Certainly not! Quite the contrary. He never said there would be no floods or fires; He only promised that in the flood we would not drown, and in the fire we would not be destroyed. To the trusting soul, these earthly afflictions are *tests*, not *catastrophes*. Viewed in true perspective, there is no conflict between 1 Peter and Psalm 91. Not only do they not conflict; they complement each other.

Our resting place and comfort are in the shadow of the Almighty. Our peace is a redemptive provision. Christ, the Deliverer, is our sure defense, and we are upheld by His power, both without and within. For many an "outer battle" is won by an "inner strength," and that inner strength is oneness with the Victor, even Jesus, our Lord. There is no fiery furnace where He is not in the midst. There is no night in which His light is not shining within the heart of His trusting children.

We are privileged to bear His name and share His reproach. In everything, whether abounding or being abased, there is a song of praise rising from the thankful heart. It is difficult to imagine a situation where the grace of God does not outweigh the severest trial. Happy is the one who has learned in everything to give thanks, knowing that in some inscrutable way, every test is in the will of God (1 Thessalonians 5:18).

To find a place to rest in turmoil is to understand Jesus asleep in the boat in the storm at sea. The only reason He needed to still the storm was to silence the fears of the disciples. The storm was not disturbing Him. I have a feeling He rather enjoyed it, for He recognized that it was from His Father's hand. If we could know that, we would not fear wind nor wave. His was the greater peace, resting *in* the storm, than that which the disciples experienced following the "miracle." (It wasn't really any more miraculous for God to stop the storm than to initiate it in the first place.) We need so much to realize that whatever befalls us within divine providence really doesn't need altering. It is we who need to be changed within—not so much the circumstances without.

If we ever come to the place where we have as much trust in the Father as Jesus had, storms will no longer frighten us. The destructive power of any enemy is dissipated by the love of God. Nothing touches the child of God except by His permissive will. *Cast all your care on Him, for He cares for you.*

Our loving heavenly Father, in the name of Jesus, our Savior, we come to the mercy seat knowing that through Him we have access to the throne of grace. Our hearts overflow with gratitude because of Thine unchangeableness, and because though all else may change Thou remainest the same forever. We can depend on Thy promises today as Abraham depended on them centuries ago. We can know Thy divine protection even as David of old knew it. We can turn to Thee in times of apparent tragedy as did the Shunammite who even in the face of death could say, "It is well."

No circumstance, however threatening, can disturb the unshakable truth of Thy faithfulness. What more can we need for peace of heart and for a song of rejoicing! We praise and magnify Thy name today and forever, and offer our hearts in loving adoration. To Thee be power and glory and majesty, for Thou art worthy. We bow in willing submission to Thy divine authority, desiring that Thy will be done in earth as in heaven, and that Thy will be done in us, Thy children, because Thou hast loved us with an everlasting love and bound us to Thyself in the bonds of Calvary. Sustain us when we falter, and forgive our sins. In Jesus' name, amen.

The Bridegroom or the Bride?

Too often we are church-conscious when we ought to be Christ-conscious. It is human nature to relate to something we can see and feel. Beloved, it isn't there: the soul rests only in God. In relating to Him is our peace and strength.

Christ died to redeem the church out of every tribe and tongue. He lives, and has always lived, in the power and majesty of all that He is, and *in Him* alone is the anchor for the soul. We do not worship the church. The *church worships Christ*, and Christ is Lord.

"Majesty sweetness sits enthroned upon the Saviour's brow; His head with radiant glories crowned, his lips with grace o'erflow." If your hope rests in the church, and your eyes are on the church, you will always be in a state of delusion, confusion, or disillusion. The church does not save you. Christ saves you. Our hope is not in a victorious church but in our victorious Lord. Our power source is *Christ*, not the church. The church's power source is Christ, not its members.

The "body" teaching can be misappropriated. It is a beautiful truth that the church is the body of Christ and that Christ loved the church and gave Himself for the church. But we do not elevate or adore the *church*. We lift up the *Head—Christ*. We look to Him who is the source of whatever grace and glory is reflected in the body. To make the body the focal point is idolatry as much as anything else we might put before Him. The fact that the church is the body of Christ does not give us liberty to glorify and elevate the church. The church is in a state of perishing the minute it focuses on itself. Cut off from its power source in Christ, the church is helpless—worse, it is *dead*.

Both the church and the kingdom have been misunderstood. We are not building the kingdom. The kingdom is not something we build. The kingdom *is*. It has been a living entity—a ruling force as long as God has been in existence, which of course is from eternity to eternity. Jesus did not come to set up the kingdom. The kingdom is synonymous with God. The kingdom is the expression of the personality and character of God. The kingdom is *God* in action. It is not waiting to be built by you and me. It is waiting to be experienced, expressed—enjoyed and demonstrated by those who are able to perceive what it is. It is waiting to be discovered—not to be created.

Jesus did not initiate the kingdom. He demonstrated it. He used the principles of the kingdom when He healed the sick, stilled the storm, raised the dead, and healed the brokenhearted. In so doing He unveiled the very heart of God, who is ever waiting to express His love to all creatures. He is bent on blessing; but in our stubborn pride we are forever bent on building. We will do something for God. Beloved, God is in need of nothing. He has already done it all for us. Man's pride ever places him in a position of patronizing God. God's love places us in the position of the sparrow and the lily of the field—receiving His benefits without labor and His provisions without merit. It is distasteful to our proud nature to be thus blessed without having performed. It is apparently equally disdainful to the church; otherwise there would not be the obvious preoccupation with accomplishments and the frenzied ambition to produce in the outer, not to mention the absence of concern for attaining and sustaining the inner strength of union in the spiritual man with the Spirit of Christ.

As long as the church is self-centered and self-concerned, it is on the decline. It is not an end in itself. It is an instrument—a channel—a vehicle for the expression of the love of God in community. It is the handprint of God in the world. It is a witness of His grace. It is the expression of His love. It is the stream of His grace; but it is not the *spring*. The *source* is ever *God* Himself. Thus the church is not to be loved, honored, and adored: Christ and Christ alone is to be honored, exalted, worshiped, and held in the supreme place of total rulership and authority. Before *Him* we bow in worship, crying, "Thou art worthy, O Lord, to receive glory and honour and power: for thou hast created all things, and for thy pleasure they are and were created" (Revelation 4:11). He is Lord of all. As has been observed, either He is Lord of all, or He is not Lord at all.

Thank God for the church. It is a marvelous mystery—the greatest force in this world for good. But it is the chariot that carries the King of kings. It is a vehicle. It is not the fullness of the Godhead. Only in *Christ* dwells all the fullness of the Godhead. Let us not deify the church. The church is not God. It is called the bride of Christ, which is precious and beautiful; but we must not idolize the bride. There is a tinge of spiritual narcissism one can detect in some religious circles where the attention is drawn more to the bride than to the Bridegroom, and this is not good. He will not share His glory. The eyes of the bride should be on her Lover—not on herself.

Some boast that they belong to *the* church. Beloved, we should be grateful to be able to confess that we belong to *the Savior*, Christ Jesus, our Lord, who purchased the church with His blood. To be a part of the church should be a matter of gratitude, not of pride, considering the price paid for our redemption. "Where is boasting then? It is excluded" (Romans 3:27). People don't need to hear about the wonderful church. They need to hear about the wonderful Savior. Jesus said, "I, if I be lifted up from the earth, will draw all men unto me" (John 12:32). He didn't say the church was to be lifted up. He said *He* was to be lifted up. Let's not confuse the issue. Pride in the church can be a reflection of pride in ourselves, and is no more acceptable to God than pride in an automobile. We must not be guilty of exalting the body over the Head, lest we make the church our Tower of Babel and end in confusion with a message nobody is able to understand. When they spoke in other tongues at Pentecost, all understood. When there was confusion of tongues at Babel, there was mass confusion.

Only as the church moves in the Spirit, honoring Christ as supreme, will the message be clear to the world, for only Christ can redeem. The church is the herald of the message—not the redeeming power. The redeeming power is *Christ*.

"I am not that Light," said John the Baptist. "I am sent to bear witness to the Light" (see John 1:8). In this respect, the church is in a similar position to John the Baptist, bearing witness to the Light—which Light is Christ. There is a lovely old hymn, "The Sands of Time Are Sinking" by Anne R. Cousin, that expresses beautifully the appropriate attitude of the church toward herself and toward her Lord:

The Bride eyes not her garment
But her dear Bridegroom's face;
I will not gaze at glory,
But on my King of grace.
Not at the crown He giveth,
But on His pierced hand,
The Lamb is all the glory
Of Immanuel's land.

Praise His name! The church will not be eulogizing herself in heaven, and whatever is going on in heaven, we do well to emulate here on earth. She will have a place of honor, sharing in His glory, but her eyes will be upon Him and her desire will be toward Him, to serve and to bring Him joy. What a privilege! We so often regret our inability to adequately praise Him here, but when freed of all that hinders, we shall be able to at last express fully the depths of our love for Him in a manner acceptable and commensurate with the magnitude of His blessings and love toward us. What a day!

There can surely be no greater achievement in this life expression than the perfection of our praise, and the more we enter into the realms of worship, the more quickly will we be loosened from whatever would hinder the growth of the soul or bind us to earthly attachments. May we be granted grace to desire this above all else and make whatever sacrifices may be needed to bring it into reality both in private worship and in group fellowship. Let our adoration be of Him and our concern be for His glory and honor.

"In the midst of the throne. . .stood a Lamb as it had been slain. . . . And they sung a new song, saying, Thou art worthy to take the book, and to open the seals thereof: for thou wast slain, and hast redeemed us to God by thy blood out of every kindred, and tongue, and people, and nation; and hast made us unto our God kings and priests: and we shall reign on the earth. And I beheld, and I heard the voice of many angels round about the throne and the beasts and the elders: and the number of them was ten thousand times ten thousand, and thousands of thousands; saying with a loud voice, Worthy is the Lamb that was slain to receive power, and riches, and wisdom, and strength, and honour, and glory, and blessing" (Revelation 5:6, 9–12).

Timely Reminders

I am crucified with Christ: nevertheless I live; yet not I, but Christ liveth in me: and the life which I now live in the flesh I live by the faith of the Son of God, who loved me, and gave himself for me" (Galatians 2:20). Therefore I will not seek to have my own will and way.

"If we walk in the light, as he is in the light, we have fellowship one with another, and the blood of Jesus Christ his Son cleanseth us from all sin" (1 John 1:7). Any righteousness we have is by the cleansing power of the blood of Jesus. "All our righteousnesses are as filthy rags" (Isaiah 64:6). Self-righteousness separates brethren. His righteousness brings us into close fellowship one with another.

Jesus is Lord. Therefore we look to *Him* for guidance and direction, and in so doing, we will not be distracted by fascinations with people, places, and things.

God is our source. "My God shall supply all your need according to his riches in glory by Christ Jesus" (Philippians 4:19). Therefore we do not need to beg and coerce other people for money. Living by faith is knowing that the God who clothes the lily will care for His own. What He does not give, we are better off not to have. "Seek ye first the kingdom of God, and his righteousness; and all these things shall be added unto you" (Matthew 6:33). (Compare Psalm 106:15.)

The Principle of Transcendency

There is a realm of glory into which I would draw you by My Spirit, saith the Lord. You have not lived in this place perpetually (as you could have done), but it has been provided for you. To live in your own thoughts is limiting, and it is so for even the wisest man. To join your mind to My mind so that your thoughts are My thoughts—this is living in the Spirit. It is a whole new kind of existence, a new orientation, new goals, new values. It is not impractical, nor does it dull your perception in the natural realm. It is an awareness superimposed on the physical plane, lifting you into the action of the Spirit of God while at the same time giving deeper meaning to earthly relationships and human values. It is a change of pace, for to move in the Spirit is to move in step with God. It is a change of complexion, for to live in the sunshine of His presence is to bring light into the darkest of earth's experiences and drive out the oppression of evil.

It was by this principle of transcendency coupled with compassion that Jesus expressed a power-filled life while He walked the earth. He was totally sensitive to both worlds, the natural and the spiritual. You may be so, too, My child, and in so doing, you will discover an almost automatic deliverance from the bondages of the carnal nature. As your desire becomes one with My desires, you will move freely and swiftly through your natural expression because you will be carried by the Spirit in all things.

Heavenly Father, in the struggles and bewilderments of life, we come to Thee, releasing all our joys and our stresses, knowing that in Thee is peace, wholeness, strength, and rest. There is wisdom in Thy Spirit sufficient to direct our every step. There is love unlimited in Thee, abounding toward all, and by Thine indwelling presence within our hearts, we have access to this flow of divine compassion so that we need not be lacking in kindness and understanding. Let Thy kingdom come in the midst of Thy people so that we may toward one another express the character of the Lord Jesus in purity and tenderness, in righteousness and in power, building faith and unity in the body of Christ. To Thee be the honor and the glory now and forever. In Jesus' name, we pray. Amen.

The Lost Gem—Humility

For ye see your calling, brethren, how that not many wise men after the flesh, not many mighty, not many noble, are called: but God hath chosen the foolish things of the world to confound the wise; and God hath chosen the weak things of the world to confound the things which are mighty; and base things of the world, and things which are despised, hath God chosen, yea, and things which are not, to bring to nought things that are: that no flesh should glory in his presence. . . . He that glorieth, let him glory in the Lord" (1 Corinthians 1:26–29, 31).

Humble? No, we are not humble. I am not, and you are not. We are told to "humble ourselves." That is because we are not humble. We may wish to be, and aspire to be, yes, and sometimes even pretend to be, but humility is not easily feigned. Furthermore, if we could succeed in humbling ourselves today, we would need to do the same again tomorrow, so fleeting is this virtue. And we do not require a reason for our pride. We are simply proud because we are proud. Nor is inferiority synonymous with humility. We may put ourselves down before another with the intent of evoking admiration for our self-abasement, but this is not humility.

We need to find the center of our being in relating to God, who is the Creator, and know that He made all things good. He deserves the credit for any good that is in us; we cannot take the credit ourselves. True humility is bowing at His feet in full recognition that all good is from His hand and to be received with gratitude and overwhelming wonder; for we know we have done nothing to merit such grace and generosity.

We are beset by pride in three basic areas: place, face, and grace. The first relates to position in life—successes, achievements, talents, status, reputation, etc. The second is the area of fashion, beauty, ornamentation, and runs the gamut of all that is designed to impress the eye of the carnal nature. The third, pride of grace, is perhaps the most grievous to the Spirit of God, for it is the most deceitful, embracing self-righteousness, religious ambition, and spiritual greed. Jesus was free of pride in every area, and by His power He can set His people free.

Humility is not a much-sought-after virtue. Humility does not appear by name in the list of the fruits of the

Spirit. It is perhaps more properly a *grace* of the spirit; for there are gifts of the Spirit, fruits of the Spirit, and graces of the Spirit—graces being attributes. The attributes of God should be manifested in His children. They embrace such things as holiness (purity), justice, truth, humility, generosity, wisdom, integrity, endurance, and power.

God is the very personification of these virtues, but if He is our Father, and we are truly His children, there should be at least a trace of the same characteristics being developed and manifested in us. The truth is that it will be on this basis that we shall one day be judged, for we are not to be judged by fame, success, or achievements, but by how much of the character of Christ is found in us.

Jesus, being the only-begotten Son of the Father, manifested these attributes. Jesus not only had a humble birth and an ignominious death: He was a humble person. Humility is an attribute of the Godhead. Pride is the hallmark of the devil. God is not proud. Pride is contradictory to His divine nature of love, grace, mercy, patience, and humility. Are we sure we understand this? We know intellectually that pride is a sin, but at the same time we have great concern for our reputation; we are hurt by criticism; we strive at all costs to "save face"; we conduct ourselves in ways designed to gain attention and approval; we dress to evoke admiration; we seek for and use possessions to impress; and we act the greater part of our lives as though pride were a virtue demanding foremost consideration rather than a vice from which we ought to flee. Jesus was motivated by none of the above attitudes, and the Son is like His Father. God is not proud, though

He alone could justly be so.

For the most part, we do not understand pride; neither do we understand humility. This fact is obvious from our behavior. It is possible that humility is indeed the crowning virtue. It is certainly the least sought after and perhaps the least desired. It is more often found in the great than in the small, and while promising nothing, it brings great reward. Without it, all the other virtues even while operating are destroyed. Yes, humility is not only the crowning virtue; it is the foundation upon which all the others rest. How can it be that we are so seldom aware when it is missing? We often realize we are impatient, stingy, ill-tempered, angry, or spiteful, and we are apt to repent and make restitution. But pride seems to have a way of hiding its identity and masquerading as something respectable, even admirable. Is it the subtlety of the ego that betrays us? And is there any remedy?

Perhaps we could gain perspective and insight by a frequent recital of the scripture "Christ Jesus came into the world to save sinners; of whom I am chief" (1 Timothy 1:15). Surely an occasional reminder of our true state might prove to be as much positive help as a flippant faith-claim of a position to which we have not by experience attained. It is all well and good to delight in the thought that "I am a child of the King." But balance is always in order, and the other side of the coin reads, "I am chief of sinners." Granted, there is a slow market for this message! Preaching the cross is not the way to win friends. But the pulpit was never meant to be a platform for a popularity contest.

When the devil wanted to tempt Jesus in the

wilderness, he took him to a high mountain and to the pinnacle of the temple. He hasn't been smart enough to change his strategies. If you ever find yourself in a high place and sitting on the pinnacle of the temple, you can be sure of one thing; it is the devil who set you there. Jesus had just received His baptism—in water and in the Holy Ghost—a twofold blessing; and He received it in a low place—in the waters of the muddy Jordan River. God delights to pour out His Spirit in *low* places. The devil will lure you to the high mountain of self-esteem and the pinnacle of self-righteousness and contrive to destroy you. Be not deceived. Prosperity, power, and false piety will rob you of the blessing you received in the Valley of Repentance. Humility is not a grace to be received and then cast aside for more auspicious gifts. Every step Jesus took led Him deeper into this Valley of Humiliation until He came to the cross. But the cross became the doorway into triumphant life and heaven's glory, and Satan's strategy was thwarted.

And so it is that a humble spirit strips the enemy of his power, for it is deaf to his promise of earthly rewards. The Spirit of Christ within you knows that you are an heir to the kingdom of heaven and that the meek shall inherit the earth. The devil can give nothing, for God is the possessor of all things. Jesus was tempted by the devil on all points of carnal desire—physical, material, and spiritual; and, beloved, we also either have been or will be tempted likewise. And what is our safeguard? It is humility.

Pride says, "Prove yourself. Prove your power, prove your success, prove your spirituality." But humility does not have need to prove anything, for it does not seek these things and thus is not lured by the temptation. Humility desires only that God shall have the glory. God doesn't need to turn stones into bread: He is the Bread. There is no reason to cast ourselves down to be caught by angels in order to prove His care: We rest at all times cradled in His everlasting arms. And why should we seek the kingdom of this world when He is King of kings and Lord of lords and has promised that we shall reign with Him in all His glory?

We can afford to wait. We can be deaf to the Tempter, for the best he can offer is a bite of poison fruit, and we shall sit down together at the marriage supper of the Lamb and drink the new wine of the kingdom of heaven.

And where do we get this power to resist the Tempter and the will to choose God's best? We get it down in the waters of baptism, where we bury our old carnal desires and rise in the newness of the life in the Spirit and receive the endowment of His power, for there is a baptism of water, and there is a baptism in the Holy Ghost. Did not John the Baptist say, "I indeed baptize you with water; but one mightier than I cometh. . .he shall baptize you with the Holy Ghost and with fire" (Luke 3:16)?

O beloved, pray that you may meet God in the waters of baptism and the power of the Holy Ghost *before* you meet the devil in the temptation of the wilderness! Otherwise, you'll never make it through. Meet Him every morning in a fresh experience of His presence and power, for you never know when a wilderness experience will come your way. It is written that "the devil left him for a season." He came back, and he'll be back for you! He'll nip at your heels until you get both of your feet through the gates of glory. But praise God, his power is limited, and even he knows his limitations. What he promises you is all a lie. He knows it is a lie. The only way he can win is if you think it is the truth. Know the Truth, love the Truth, desire the Truth, and the Truth will set you free. The Truth will be your protection, for the Truth is God Himself.

Heavenly Father, shower upon us the refreshing dew of Thy
Holy Spirit, and give us a new baptism of holy love and fire.
Burn away the chaff of distracting thoughts, and center our
hearts upon Thyself. Cut us loose from things that hinder the
flow of your power. Lift us above the pettiness of self-love and
the soul-destroying treachery of pride. We long to be more like
Jesus in His tenderness and compassion. Let your grace be like a
river, Lord, flowing through our limitations and moving us out
into Thy fullness. In Jesus' name, we pray. Amen.

The Balancing Factor

What is the motivating force of your life? What is your goal? Why do you make the choices and follow the paths that lead you into new experiences? Where are you going, and why?

These are questions we need to ask ourselves, and the more frequently, the better. It would help protect us from going off on tangents. The Spirit of God is ever present with us to be a balancing factor. God's Word is filled with words of caution as well as with magnificent promises. We love to memorize and quote the promises. It would serve us well to match every promise with a commandment. We ought to be as concerned about developing godly character as we are about receiving blessings. Perhaps godly character is the greatest blessing we could ever receive. We would do well to give equal attention to the whole message of the Bible, not neglecting the sterner words that contain

God's standard of conduct, His precepts and laws by which we are constrained to live. These are very specific, and very practical, and they were by no means swept away by the cross.

There are more commandments in the New Testament than there are in the Old. Being religious does not waive the divine intention of righteousness: the accountability that is put upon us to maintain right conduct. A thousand prayers do not atone for a dishonest heart. A lifetime of preaching will not blot out a vicious temper. To proclaim love for God and scorn a brother is a travesty. God desires truth in the inner man. It is the desire of the Spirit of God to do a work in our spirit so that our outer life and our inner life will be consistent. He will not rest until this is accomplished. It could be hastened by a greater degree of understanding and cooperation on our part. We can allow Him to do His corrective, creative work in us to bring us into conformity with the image of Christ, or we can cling to our sins in self-deception and live and die a spiritual cripple, never entering into the riches of His grace and the power of His Spirit to produce His holiness in us and make us overcomers.

Let us beware lest we fall, having thought we were standing. "Let him that thinketh he standeth take heed lest he fall" (1 Corinthians 10:12). We will never stand in our own righteousness, for that is as filthy rags. Left to ourselves, we will boast of our most glaring faults. It is only at the foot of the cross, in the light of Calvary, that we shall be given the insight to see ourselves in the true light of His sacrifice, and cry out, as did Job, "I abhor myself, and repent in dust and ashes" (Job 42:6).

We come into Thy presence, O Lord, knowing that truly Thou art our only source of life and peace. Without Thee our souls would be parched and our hearts would fail. It is Thy strength that upholds us from day to day. It is Thy love that eases the stress of earthly cares and adds beauty to the drabbest pathway. We can rejoice in all things, recognizing Thy presence with us and seeing by faith Thine eternal purposes rising above the shadows of our struggles and our disappointments. Give us the courage to faithfully follow Thee wheresoever Thou dost lead, for Thy sake and for Thy glory. In Jesus' precious name, we pray. Amen.

A Psalm of Praise

O my God, make no tarrying. Come unto me; for Thou art my habitation; Thou art my dwelling place. In Thee only has my soul found rest. From everlasting to everlasting, Thou art God. From eternity to eternity, Thou alone remainest steadfast. Thou alone art true. Thou alone art holy, and Thou art above all and in all, and in Thee do all things consist.

Thou art the author of all true blessing, the fountain of all true joy. Thou and Thou alone art worthy to be praised, for Thy name above all others is glorious. Thou art majesty and grace combined.

Surely the heavens show forth Thy handiwork, and the lilies of the field Thy tender care. Thou art mindful of all Thy creation and givest to all in due season. Thou art not slack concerning Thy promises. Thou art slow to wrath and ready to forgive. I cried unto Thee, and Thou answeredst me. Thou hast delivered me in the hour of great need and wast near me to comfort me.

Thy love sustained me, Thy grace upheld me, and by Thy power were mine enemies subdued. Thou art my rock and my salvation. Thou art the strength of my life, mine everlasting portion and delight.

My heart is overwhelmed within me at the remembrance of Thy goodness; yea, my tongue faileth me when I would speak Thy praise. Let me not depart from Thy presence. Let me abide in Thy tabernacle all the days of my life.

We come into Thy presence, our loving heavenly Father, through the merits of the shed blood of our Lord Jesus Christ, knowing that even as we approach the mercy seat, it is the Holy Spirit who makes intercession for us. We ask Thy forgiveness for our sins and transgressions. We are helpless and needy, but we remember Thy word: "Let the weak say I am strong." Thou, O Lord, art our strength, and in the Spirit we are seated with Thee in the heavenlies. We accept it in faith and rest in the finished work of redemption, knowing we are brought near to Thee by the blood, and nothing we could ever do could add to the perfectness of our Savior's sacrifice.

We accept our forgiveness with praise and gratitude, and ask Thy grace that we may in like manner forgive our brother, being mindful that we have been required to forgive our brother first, and then to come to Thine altar. Bless those in authority, bless Thy children, and bless all men everywhere, and may we yet see the fulfillment of the prophecy of Joel, "I will pour out My Spirit upon all flesh," to Thine honor and glory. In Jesus' name, we pray. Amen.

Lord of Kings

The One whom we serve is in authority over rulers. He is *Lord of kings*. Kings may rule over their kingdoms, but there is One who rules over them: It is the *King* of kings and the *Lord* of lords. Shall He not, then, rule over us, His children? Shall He not exercise control over our lives and our actions? If we are threatened by the thought, we are ignorant of His purposes and wise in our own conceits. To invite His control is to safeguard our spirits from destruction. To recognize that He desires to rule over us and will do so with diligence and integrity and love is the basic requirement for activating His authoritative power in our lives. What vast blessings we forfeit when we insist on holding this power ourselves! In the final end, He will rule us anyway; but what about this present moment? Can we not benefit greatly by invoking His control in all our daily living?

Do you want to break the tyranny of other people's wills controlling your life? This is the secret. Give the control deliberately and decisively to Christ, and know that anyone who injects himself into that place is invading holy ground. We are to guard our spirits as a king would guard his castle, indeed, even more so, because our spirits are the very source of our life force. Without a full supply of the power that comes from direct contact with the Holy Spirit and unbroken communion, the child of God today cannot survive the spiritual warfare in which he finds himself engulfed. Contrary winds are blowing, and powers of darkness are active. Only Christ is able to save, and we place ourselves outside His protecting grace when we refuse to come under His sovereign control. He will not force it upon us. He is a King, to be sure, but He is not a tyrant. His rulership in this day of grace is the rule of love. It is still Calvary love as deep and as pure as it was two thousand years ago. Have we grown too callous or too sophisticated to respond? Can we find a place of repentance and of brokenness? Can we humble ourselves and seek His mercy and His forgiveness? May it be so.

Our Father, we look to Thee for the supply of our needs, for Thou art the source of all good. In Thee is our peace, our safety, our strength, and our supply. Our hearts are at rest knowing Thou hast promised to care for us as we cast our burdens upon Thee. Teach us more perfectly to do this so that we are not weighed down with needless anxiety. Make us a people who have learned how to rejoice in all things and praise Thee in every circumstance, knowing that Thou dost see and wilt undertake for us in those things that are beyond our power to change. Bless, we pray, all who are in places of severe stress. Grant Thy peace that passes understanding that they may be comforted. In Jesus' name, we pray. Amen.

Angels of Mercy

My little one, you are precious to Me, and I am ever at your side to bring strength and comfort, wisdom and guidance. You are a vessel prepared for My glory. You should be filled with My spirit at all times. To do this, there must be a release of the things that cause you stress. It is not a laying aside of responsibility, but a refusal of anxiety. You cannot serve Me well under tension, for My life is a free-flowing stream. My way is not burdensome. When life is a burden, it is your burden, not Mine. You can lay it down yourself, because you are the one who picked it up. You can pick up My peace at any point just like you picked up the burden. It is a matter of choice. You can be happy, or you can be sad. You can express faith, or you can voice anxiety. Faith and joy are of My Spirit; worry and depression are of your own making. You create the atmosphere around your soul by your choice of position. You are always either *in Christ* or in yourself. To be in yourself is to be in constant conflict. You are tuning in the world and receiving static. Tune in to My Spirit and you will hear music—the heavenly harmony of My love and My purity. There is no place for worry in My presence. Every time you worry, you turn off the music and produce discord. It is when you broadcast that discord that you drive from you those I have sent to help.

I have sent you angels of mercy. You can trust them as you would trust Me, for they are My channels of blessing to you. They are sent to help you, and you can trust yourself to their hands. They shall "bear you up in their hands," as the Bible says. This you need. I know your need. I know you need help. I have provided the help you need, but you have not recognized it. You have thought to yourself, "This is a man." No, this is not a man—this is an angel: My angel of mercy sent to bless you. Trust Me, and trust the instruments I have chosen to use to help you. I will protect you from harm, for I am in complete control. You have caused yourself unnecessary worry. Put yourself in the big circle of My presence, and your problem will become a tiny speck on the outside. You will restore perspective. You will regain your peace, and you will find joy; for it is not your joy: It is My joy, and I give it to you. Nothing can destroy *My joy*! Forget your sorrow. Let it go. Take My joy, and take it in its fullness. It is impossible to be too happy.

Visit us, O Holy Spirit, with a fresh outpouring of Thy loving grace. Though we walk in hard places, there is inner peace and outer rejoicing because we know that we have a caring heavenly Father and a faithful Friend, even Christ Jesus, our Lord. Never are we alone, and never are we forsaken. We stand secure and rest in the confidence of Thy never-failing mercies. Teach us how to abide in the secret place of communion and devotion. In Jesus' name, we pray. Amen.

Of No Reputation

It is written of Jesus that He "made Himself of no reputation." Such a concept is foreign to our ears in this day of empire building, self-esteem, and self-promotion. Even when He was introduced by John the Baptist, He was described as the "Lamb of God"—the slain lamb, actually, for John said, "Behold the Lamb of God, which taketh away the sin of the world" (John 1:29). And so He was presented as not only the Lamb, but the *sacrificial lamb*. In the mind of God, He very truly was "born crucified," and in His own heart He was at all times aware of this.

We talk about dying to the flesh and laying aside our own will that we may more perfectly please God and fulfill His desires. Beloved, Jesus never knew any other way. He entered this world totally committed and never wavered from that dedication. We read of Him in Philippians 2:5–8, "Let this mind be in you, which was also in Christ Jesus: who, being in the form of God, thought it not robbery to be equal with God: but *made himself of no reputation*, and took upon him the form of a *servant*, and was made in the likeness of men: and being found in fashion as a man, he humbled himself, and became obedient unto death, even the death of the cross."

Jesus had no purpose other than to please His Father. Everything He expressed toward men was in the interest of furthering the kingdom of heaven, which is to say carrying out His purposes and implementing His laws, which are designed for man's ultimate benefit.

Can it be that He was "despised and rejected of men; a man of sorrows, and acquainted with grief" perhaps for this very reason? Would He have been more welcome, more popular, more admired and sought after if He had been born as many anticipated He would be, in royal splendor and in palatial surroundings? If He had been announced as the King of kings and displayed His excellence by wearing a golden crown and purple robes, would He have received the devotion and respect of the people?

This leads us to the scripture that says, "I am come in my Father's name, and ye receive me not: if another shall come in his own name, him ye will receive" (John 5:43). Jesus is saying that He came not making or trying to make a reputation for Himself or claiming anything of Himself, but when the Antichrist comes, he will come with pomp and glory, displaying his power and assuming great authority, and man will receive him gladly. Why? Because it is inherent in human nature to respond in a positive way to a personality displaying self-confidence, power, leadership qualities, and aggressiveness. We are made of that kind of stuff. Power impresses us; glamour fascinates us; wealth hypnotizes us; and we are soon out of touch with the real values of life, and certainly out of harmony with the Spirit of God.

The world did not want a meek and lowly person. They questioned the credibility of a king who was born in a stable with no credentials of nobility. Out of a framework of obscurity, poverty, and humility, Jesus went about His Father's business. There was no demand for recognition. He never put anybody down in order to put Himself up. If there were complaints against Him, they were freely expressed—to His face. Have you ever tried to do that to a proud person? He was so approachable that all sorts of people felt perfectly free to confront Him with their disapproval of His actions, to challenge His authority, and to reprove Him for what in their eyes were His faults. In reading the Gospels, it becomes very apparent that the majority of people were displeased with Him. He crossed their wills. He failed to fulfill their personal expectations. He was calm when they were disturbed, and they were irritated. He ignored traditions they held sacred. He unmasked their hypocrisy. He exposed their greed. He forgave sins and healed people they rejected and avoided. He caused embarrassment by His persistent disregard for protocol—religious protocol in particular.

In times of stress it is helpful to remember that, like Jesus, we are here to do the Father's will and to please Him. It would be nice if we could also please everyone else, but all too often we are placed in a position where we have to choose—to please the Father or to please people. And it takes more than choosing: it takes courage. The way of the cross is not for cowards, weaklings, or lazy people. It is not for the double-minded or for the insincere. We may never have to die for Jesus, but we do have to count our lives as nothing in order to give priority to the doing of His will. The only alternative to living according to His commandments is to make our own rules, and if we make our own rules that are contrary to His nature and desires, we place ourselves outside His providential blessings.

We are born into God's family through faith in the finished work of Christ; we are heirs to the kingdom, sons of God, and dear to the heart of the Father. But although by position we are thus exalted, it behooves us to take voluntarily a place of servants and slaves that we may serve Him in humility. Submission is the order of the day. We are speaking not of privileges but of attitudes. True, we shall reign with Him, and in a sense we already do reign with Him. But He is sovereign and Lord, and our spirit should bend in willing submission to His authority. A haughty attitude is inappropriate. Jesus was Lord of the universe, but He was gentle and tender of spirit. He could have descended on the wicked with holy vengeance. He could have called down fire out of heaven to consume the dens of iniquity; instead, He went about doing good. Romans 12:21 reads, "Be not overcome of evil, but overcome evil with good." The book of Jude describes in detail the sins of the wicked; and what is the concluding word of admonition to the believers? It is found in verses 20–21: "But ye, beloved, building up yourselves on your most holy faith, praying in the Holy Ghost, keep yourselves in the love of

God, looking for the mercy of our Lord Jesus Christ unto eternal life." And the writer adds the conclusion in verses 24–25: "Now unto him that is able to keep you from falling, and to present you faultless before the presence of his glory with exceeding joy, to the only wise God our Saviour, be glory and majesty, dominion and power, both now and ever. Amen."

What shall we do when evil abounds? "Keep yourselves in the love of God." What shall we do when persecution comes? "Build yourselves up on your most holy faith by praying in the Holy Ghost." What shall we do when testings and trials and temptations come? We shall remember that God is able to keep us from falling and to present us faultless before the presence of His glory with exceeding joy. Praise His name!

*We come into Thy presence, our Father, to praise Thy holy name
and to thank Thee from hearts that overflow with gratitude
for all Thy goodness. Thou art worthy, for Thou hast conquered
every power of evil and hast taken authority over all the works
of darkness. We await the day when Thy glory shall fill the earth
and every knee shall bow to Thy dominion. Hasten that time,
we pray; and meanwhile, we pray that in our own hearts, as we
yield our wills to Thine, Thou wilt subdue every evil influence
that would rise against our souls. Let us experience victory over
the enemy through the power of the indwelling Holy Spirit.
Give us boldness to witness, and may we walk in love and
possess our souls in patience. In Jesus' name, we pray. Amen.*

Take Heart!

O child of God, take heart! Be encouraged, for I am
working on your behalf to bring to pass that for which you
have been earnestly contending in prayer. Your petitions
have come before Me, and I am moved by the need. No
situation is so difficult that I am unable to help; neither is
any request too insignificant to be granted.

Hold fast your confidence. Wait upon Me. I will surely
perform it. Rebuke anxiety. Praise Me *now*. In so doing,
you will have a double victory; for faith carries a reward all
its own, quite apart from the blessing of answered prayer.
Praise also is a benefit in itself, especially in the face of
perplexity or adversity; for praise and faith are virtues of the
soul, and as such are of supreme value.

Work—yes. Serve Me—yes. But more than these, *love Me*. Otherwise I am lost in the serving and I have no longer a heart-interest in your work. Be not overcome in the process of resisting evil. Let your soul be filled with Me, and the good that is part of Myself will of its own power overcome evil.

I am the Lord your God who loves you and delights in you. Yes, I shall rest in My love, and My heart shall be at leisure with your heart. I will help you as you trust Me.

I will walk in your midst and will share the burden with you. I will encourage you and strengthen you, and will show you My mighty power in proportion to your faith.

We come to Thee, O Lord, with praise and thanksgiving for Thy boundless love. We cannot fathom Thy majesty, but we bow in humble adoration before Thee and offer to Thee all that we have to bring—the gratitude of our hearts. Forgive the many times when we have been unmindful of Thy goodness and when we have taken for granted Thy mercy and protection. How often Thou hast spared us from destruction and we have been unaware. How often, when we have wandered like the prodigal, Thou hast waited patiently for our return. Forgive us, Lord, our thoughtlessness, and give us eyes to see the depths of Thy grace, and hearts responsive to Thy love. In Jesus' name, amen.

The Creative Power of the Love of God

In the midst of turmoil, there is peace for you, My child, in the shadow of My wings. It is not that I have deserted you when storms rise; neither is it that you have left Me. Relationship is not altered by trouble. Trouble does not indicate My disfavor. It comes to all. Grace prevails in an atmosphere of trust. To question My love in the time of adversity is the worst thing you can do. Your greatest help lies in affirming the changelessness of our union. By keeping your confidence in Me intact, you are sure to rise above every adverse situation and break through to victory.

It is not an absence of conflict that creates spiritual poise; it is, rather, tenacious faith in the face of odds. It is a deepening of your love for Me that I desire. If you share this desire with Me, you will not flinch when the way is hard. It was hard for Me also—much harder than it will ever be for you. Draw your strength from My faithfulness and your courage from My love. Be not afraid. Faith countenances no fear. *Faith banks on eternal verities and views the highest mountain as a straw in the wind.*

The love of God is a creative power that defies all the forces of darkness. It (the creative power of the love of God) is never inactive: It is brought into operation in any given circumstance by the faith of the believer. It is all that is needed to change defeat to victory. It is a dynamic joy bomb, and as its power is released, it will shatter the forces of resistance and open the way for advance.

You can lay aside your own strategy like a child's toy. It is useless and worthless. I have a higher plan of action—a frontal attack against the enemy. Set your eyes on Me and disregard the problem. *I am the answer. I am more than able.*

Lay hold upon My character. It is a shelter in every calamity. It will preserve you through this one, and you can come forth singing. If you really want to please Me, you will start now, and you will continue until faith prevails for all concerned; for I will use *your faith* to build the faith of others. You have been looking for an answer to prayer when you should have been seeking My face for greater faith. Your *faith* will generate the supply.

Give us, heavenly Father, the courage and the humility to allow Thy Holy Spirit to search us out, to try us, and to see if there be any evil way in us. For Jesus' sake, we pray. Amen.

God Is Not Delinquent

I have been young, and now am old," said the psalmist, "yet have I not seen the righteous forsaken, nor his seed begging bread" (Psalm 37:25). Beloved, something is wrong when a true believer cannot honorably meet his financial obligations, and on time. God is not unfaithful. He has promised that He will meet all our needs according to His riches in glory, and this includes financial needs. To be irresponsible in financial matters is to cast a shadow on the promises of God and His ability to care for His own. If He clothes the lilies of the field, will He not also clothe you? If He feeds the sparrow, will He let you go hungry? No, the problem is not in the integrity of God, but in the lack of integrity in man.

The man who cannot pay his bills is either living beyond his means or misappropriating funds. Either one is tantamount to robbing the individuals who have prior claim to the assets, which claim they rightfully have because of services already rendered by the free choice of the debtor. The world owes you nothing: You owe the world. To seek refuge in rationalizations is to avoid the issue and indulge in falsification of the facts. "God understands," you may say. No, God does not understand any conduct that springs from selfish disregard for the proper rights of others. Jesus paid the debt for your sins on the cross, but the responsibilities of one man to another man are the sole responsibility of man. God will help you meet your obligations if you are honest. If you owe your brother fifty dollars and you take that fifty dollars and buy a pair of shoes, you cannot expect God to give you another fifty dollars to pay your debt. If you pay your debt *first*, God will not let you go barefooted. The grace of God does not put us beyond the implications of the Ten Commandments, one of which is "Thou shalt not steal." First things first. Bills take priority over expenditures.

God never puts anything on us that is not intended for our own good and our best interests. He does not "saddle" us with burdensome requirements. "Honesty is the best policy" has its roots in the Bible, for God told His people that if they wanted to have a good and a prosperous life, they should keep His commandments. Deuteronomy 5:29: "O that there were such an heart in them, that they would fear me, and keep all my commandments always, that it might be well with them, and with their children for ever!" And verse 33: "Ye shall walk in all the ways which the LORD your God hath commanded you, that ye may live. . .and that ye may prolong your days in the land which ye shall possess." That was for Israel, you say? Yes, it was for Israel, and it is for you and me. God's precepts and laws do not change. By dishonesty we hurt our own selves, and we damage our children by the bad example.

Straightforward? Yes, because we need to face up to basic facts and line up our lives by God's standard of moral conduct. Anything less than total honesty will cripple your spiritual relationship with Christ no matter how religious you may consider yourself to be. This message needs to be restated, because much laxity has crept into the lives of many professing Christians, and it is glossed over by extravagant claims of looking for miracles, living by faith, and other pious delusions, all designed to cover up our intrinsic selfishness and our greed for the things of this world for our own self-gratification and pride. Let's stop fooling ourselves (for we are not fooling other people)! It is much easier to be faithful at the prayer meeting than it is to pay our bills. Remember the scripture that says, in effect, if you have something that needs to be made right with a brother, don't stay at the altar to pray, but go to your brother and first make that thing right, and *then* you can pray! Revivals do not necessarily begin in church. More often they begin when we make things right with our fellow man, in accordance with the laws of God, which call for honesty and justice and consideration of the rights of others.

Romans 12:17 reads, "Provide things honest in the sight of all men." Hebrews 13:18 tells us, "Pray for us: for we trust we have a good conscience, in all things willing to live honestly." And there is 1 Thessalonians 4:6: "That no man go beyond and defraud his brother in any matter: because that the Lord is the avenger of all such, as we also have forewarned you and testified." Remember that while the Holy Spirit is comforting you, God is keeping a record of your financial affairs, and there is coming a day of reckoning, and indeed, it may come sooner than you think! We need to put our house in order and speedily.

This message is directed to those who feel no particular commitment to financial responsibility. If you are making an honest effort to meet your obligations, it is not for you. You can pass it on to someone you think may need it, or keep it to bolster your own determination not to be lured into the all-too-popular trend toward fascination with luxuries not included when Jesus promises to supply all our need and to feed us with our daily bread—one day at a time. He says in effect, "Take no thought for what you will eat or wear tomorrow, because it is enough to cope with the problems of today." (See Matthew 6:24–34.)

It is time for sanity and simplicity, both of which are rapidly vanishing from modern society. And the problem is not the inflated economy nor our deflated bank accounts. The problem is our "wanter"—we *want* too much. What we *need* is the gift of gratitude to displace our sickness of greed, and some contentment with what we already possess to displace our resentment concerning what we have not yet acquired. "The world is too much with us. Getting and spending, we lay waste our powers," wrote the poet.

There is nothing new about this problem. Meeting obligations was never enjoyable. We enjoy living in a house; we do not particularly enjoy paying rent or taxes. We enjoy riding in a car; we do not enjoy paying for gas. We enjoy good food; we do not enjoy paying the grocery bill.

"Times are hard," we say. They always were. They are hard in inflation and in depression. They are "hard" because we can never have all the things we want. The more we want things we can't afford to have, the "harder" the times seem to be. The harder we work, the more we earn, the more we want, and the more we spend. The idea of saving for the things we want has been eliminated by the credit card system, and the consequent illusion that all things are now within reach. This illusion is shattered only when the eventual bills exceed the income, at which time we are encouraged to seek a new loan to pay the old debts and further compound our problems, with no relief anywhere in sight.

Beloved, nothing takes God by surprise. The Bible is always contemporary. Jesus gave us the formula for financial peace and success when He said, "Seek ye first the kingdom of God, and His righteousness; and all these things shall be added unto you" (Matthew 6:33). God wants our needs to be supplied. He is loving, good, and generous; but He has a way for us to be prosperous: *It is to love Him—not things.* It is to make Him *Lord*, put Him first, and learn the joy of *giving—* first to Him, and then to others.

Our Lord and Savior, in these days of testings and trials, we would learn to rest beneath Thy wings of mercy and draw strength and courage from the knowledge of Thine eternal unchangeableness. Though all about us is in a state of passing away and there is no certainty in this life, there is an anchor that holds steady in Thine immutable promises and in Thy holy character. We find our consolation in Thine abiding presence and draw our strength from Thy precious Word. May Thy praise be continually on our lips and Thy love flood our hearts. In Jesus' name, we pray. Amen.

Holiness and Grace— Inseparable Companions

If love is as a sweet fragrance, *grace* is a garden of spices. Grace has a seasoning quality and preserving properties. The depths of grace can never be plumbed; the breadth of grace can never be measured. Grace is God's love in operation, reaching out to embrace the wretched sinner. It is God's mercy reaching down and lifting the sinking soul out of the quicksand of his miserable failures. It is the divine intervention of the Redeemer dispelling the powers of evil to rescue the defeated out of the pit of remorse and to lift him into the Father's forgiveness. *Grace*—the theme of countless songs and poems and the inspiration for endless sermons and books.

As an old hymn puts it, "Grace, 'tis a charming sound, harmonious to the ear; heav'n with the echo shall resound, and all the earth shall hear. Saved by grace alone! This is all my plea: Jesus died for all mankind, and Jesus died for me."

Grace is the primary and the ultimate remedy for our ills, but we try everything else first. Grace restores, but we prevent its effectual work by attempting to bind our own wounds. No matter how far we run from God or how deep our need, His *grace* is there. "Thou compassest my path and my lying down, and art acquainted with all my ways. . . . If I make my bed in hell, behold, thou art there. . . . If I say, Surely the darkness shall cover me; even the night shall be light about me. . . . When I awake, I am still with thee" (Psalm 139:3, 8, 11, 18).

We can never escape Him, for He is not only round about; He is *within*, and His *grace* is active at all times, whether recognized or not. It is like the air we breathe: We could not exist without it, but we take it for granted, presume upon it, and give it no thought under normal circumstances. This is what we do with God's *grace*. It is the environment within which we are able to survive spiritually, but too often we are oblivious to its life-sustaining quality, and because we are not more consciously aware of its contribution to our spiritual well-being, we limit its power to bless us in full measure. To the measure to which we limit its power, in like measure are we impoverished.

If we could but grasp the true scope of *grace*, our Christian experience would be infinitely enhanced. Through the imputation of the righteousness of Christ, the believer is in a *position* of holiness before God. By *position*, he is a saint. But by *experience*, he falls short of the glory of God, thus needing the *grace* of God continually to make his salvation effectual. The Bible tells us, "Without holiness no man shall see God"; and we are commanded to *be perfect* as He is perfect. This is a stringent standard. Who can attain? It is at the point of this dilemma where we find the reality of what we are (continually falling short of the glory of God) and *what we are enjoined to be* (perfect) that the *grace* of God (the extension of His love and mercy in the face of our unworthiness) operates to rescue the trusting child of God, holding him in a place of favor in the eyes of the Father when he would otherwise be a castaway. If your concept of salvation leaves no room for the grace of God to be operative in the face of man's imperfection, you have a rigid, legalistic standard of righteousness that will permit none but the wholly sanctified, perfectly pure in heart, totally victorious, sinless individual to enter the Father's house. Beloved, if such were the case, heaven would be a place where God dwells in utter solitude, lamenting the total failure of His redemptive plan and grieving over the cost of Calvary in the face of its utter ineffectuality. Thank God, this is not the case.

When we confess our sins and accept the Lord Jesus Christ as personal Savior, all the record of past sins is blotted out, and we are "accepted in the Beloved." His *righteousness* is put to our account: We are as near and as dear to God as is His Son, for we are joint heirs with Him in all the riches of the kingdom of heaven. Now, righteousness is a wonderful thing. It means right relationship to God in holiness. But righteousness is not to be equated with *character*. The righteousness of Christ is "put upon you" (imputed); but *character* is worked *in* you, and this is a *process* and requires time and effort: It is not a *gift*. It is the process called in theological language *sanctification*. It is the working out of that which has been put in. His divine life has been implanted within us in the salvation experience—in the new birth miracle. From that point on, it is the work of the indwelling Holy Spirit, working in conjunction with the desire of the believer to bring about an inner and outer transformation of the entire life expression so that it will be a true reflection of the personality of Jesus. It is the "old things passing away, and all things becoming new." It is renewing the mind to conform to the mind of Christ in purity. It is turning the back on the sinful habit patterns of the unregenerate nature, and cultivating holy thoughts and purposes in harmony with the very heart of God, the Father. It is relinquishing selfishness in preference to doing the will of One whose only desire is to love and to bless. It is a life of becoming Christlike—in every aspect of our daily expression—in feeling, thinking, and doing.

Sanctification is a continual birthing into newness in holiness and purity, and the process goes on from here to eternity. Someone has said, "Show me a man who professes to be perfect, and let me ask his wife." Perfection is something we are *after*—not something we have attained. Only God is totally good. The golden bridge that connects the goal toward which we press and the place wherein we find ourselves is the *grace* of God.

There are as many divergent ideas about this teaching as there are trees in a forest. Theologians have pondered it and argued over it more than they have puzzled over the age of the earth or the details of our Lord's return. This is not an attempt to set forth the ultimate solution. It is only an appeal to dust off God's Word, take a fresh look at the precious truths of His boundless love and mercy, and hopefully free some overburdened soul from the bondages of legalism and the burden of guilt. "There is therefore now no condemnation to them which are in Christ Jesus, who walk not after the flesh, but after the Spirit" (Romans 8:1).

Why? Because they are *perfect*? No! Because of the *grace of God*!

> *Grace taught my soul to pray,*
> *And made mine eyes o'erflow;*
> *'Twas grace which kept me to this day,*
> *And will not let me go.*
> —Augustus M. Toplady
> "Grace, 'Tis a Charming Sound"

Our Father and our God, we cast ourselves upon Thy mercy, for without Thee we have no hope. In Thee are hidden all the riches of grace, and through faith, and faith alone, we lay hold upon Thy promises. Cleanse us from all unrighteousness, and forgive us for every thought and action by which we have grieved Thy Holy Spirit. We place all within us under the shed blood of Jesus, and pray for Thy healing touch for body, soul, and spirit. We thank Thee for hearing us. In Jesus' name, we pray. Amen.

Christh Our Righteousness

There is, unfortunately, a great disparity between *what we are* and *what God is*, in terms of holiness. We are called to holiness. We are taught by the Word of God the importance, the standard, the divine intention in regard to holiness. God is holy. God desires that we, His children, shall be like Him in holiness. He desires to fellowship with us and for us to share eternity with Him in a holy place. It is written that nothing that defiles shall enter there.

We need to understand what God means when He speaks of holiness and to examine our hearts in the light of His Word to see if we have any holiness by His standards, and finally, if we do not have it, to find out if there is any possible way that we can get it.

First of all, we must have honesty. We must face up to the fact that we do not posses *anything* by merely *wishing* that we have it, nor do we have anything by making a false claim of possession when it is nowhere in concrete evidence. God wants us to be holy, and we may desire to be holy, but that does not make it so. Claiming something we do not actually manifest is self-deceptive.

To be holy, we must be totally and consistently rid of sin—all sin. But the Word tells us we are all continually falling short of the glory of God. All are imperfect by God's standard of perfection, and all are in a process of being made conformable to the image of God in Christ, and none have perfectly realized the fullness of His redemptive, sanctifying work. ("All" here is of course referring to born again believers.)

So we are in a dilemma. Shall we despair, or shall we press on? Shall we compare ourselves to others and measure our degree of holiness in terms of the relative and find satisfaction in contrasting our own level of goodness against the total depravity of the unregenerate? Shall we take God's standard of apparent unattainable perfection and move it down within our reach one way or another? Shall we fabricate a standard on our own terms?

Any honest, sincere child of God must surely recognize that in the light of God's pure, holy character and expression, he is miles and miles from his desired destination in terms of personal perfection. Any who loudly proclaim to the contrary are misinformed, misguided, and self-deceived, no matter how good they are. "None is good, save God," said Jesus.

Then you may say, What is the use? Why try? Why strive for the impossible? Or why should we reproach ourselves for not being able to successfully produce something we are incapable of producing? Is God unreasonable in His demands, or can He be induced to make some sort of compromise in order to rescue us out of a hopeless situation?

This is by no means a hypothetical question. This is a very real problem to the thinking child of God. On the one hand, he knows he is expected to be perfect. On the other hand, he is very painfully aware that he most certainly is *not*, unless he chooses deliberately to deceive himself and to simply claim to be something other than what he is.

Is our wise, loving heavenly Father oblivious to our struggle? No indeed! He anticipated it and made full provision through the gift of His indwelling Holy Spirit. Therein lies the secret of victory over sin: The Perfect One in all His authority and power to take dominion over sin lives within to produce in us the holiness we cannot of ourselves attain. He is our righteousness. He is our purity. He is our peace. He is our life. Christ in us is our hope of glory. Christ in us is loving, kind, patient, forgiving, longsuffering, temperate, pure—full of joy, hope, and faith. What is impossible for us is possible for Him. He has come to *abide* and also to *manifest* Himself through us. His love is shed abroad in our hearts and radiates forth to others. His Spirit has taken residency within us in order to empower us to do works of righteousness and bring forth fruit that will reflect a redemptive work.

This is God's answer to our helplessness. Knowing our total inability to produce any true righteousness of our own, God said in effect, We will come down and do it in you, for you, and through you. All you have to do is believe, receive, yield, and *let* (allow). It is the simplicity of trusting, resting, and allowing Christ to live out His life in and through us. In the words of the apostle Paul: "I am crucified with Christ: nevertheless *I live*; yet *not I*, but *Christ liveth in me*: and the life which I now live in the flesh I live by the faith of the Son of God, who loved me, and gave himself for me. I do not frustrate the grace of God: for if righteousness come by the law, then Christ is dead in vain" (Galatians 2:20–21). It is only in *letting Him* live His life through us that His true spirit of holiness will ever be real in our experience and expression.

Blessed Savior, we kneel at the foot of Thy cross and lay down our heavy burden. We have nothing to bring Thee except our need. We have no gift to offer and no merit to plead. Hear our cry, and be merciful to us Thy children. Apart from Thee there is no hope. Without Thy redeeming grace we are helpless to save ourselves. Look upon us with favor because of Thy sacrifice, for Thou through Thine atoning death hast purchased for us eternal life. Accept our gratitude, Lord Jesus, we pray. Amen.

The Great Physician

I am not good, and you are not good: *Jesus is good*, and whatever goodness ever manifest in you or in me will be only as and when and if He by His Spirit and by His power is producing the fruit of righteousness in our lives. In this we should rejoice, for what is difficult for us is easy and natural for Him. All the unlovely aspects of our natural dispositions can be put under the blood of Jesus, and all His loveliness and beauty can be allowed to flourish instead. The striving and the struggling are useless. It is the *letting* that brings it most quickly to reality. Fleshly determination to "be good" will end in defeat. Religious exercises of the sort that gender self-righteousness are a further hindrance. You will never produce the Christlike life: *He is going to do it in you.* We will be most helped by exposing our spirits to His influence, through the Word of God, through prayer, meditation, contemplation, and adoration.

Love is miracle-working power, and the free-flowing

exchange of our love to Him and His love to us is like a pure, crystal river cleansing our souls and bringing refreshing and life. Once you find that river of free-flowing fellowship with the Lord, you will never again complain of a "desert-place" experience. If your soul feels dry, it is because you are tangled up in yourself, trying to find your answers within yourself. It is a futile search. Settle it once for all that in yourself you are nothing, *in Christ you are all things*, and in between His grace sustains, for His love will not let you utterly destroy yourself in your ignorance.

Are you languishing in a place of seeming hopelessness, bemoaning your lack of consistency, wondering why you cannot always be on the mountaintop, praising God and rejoicing, going from victory to victory as you suppose a "normal" Christian ought to be doing? I have good news for you, or rather, God has good news for you! He is also in the valley of discouragement and in the shadows of despair. He is in isolation as well as in convocation. He is as near to the seemingly defeated as He is to the celebrant. God sees you, as His trusting child, through the cleansing blood of Jesus, and His love for you is undaunted by your struggles.

Grace is divine favor showered upon the undeserving. Beloved, you do not have to *earn* God's love. He is not an implacable tyrant. It is unfortunate indeed that we should ever transfer to God the type of personality we so often are confronted with in men—particularly religious men. Rigidity and condemnation are not components of God's grace. There is a world of difference between the incisive conviction of the Holy Spirit dealing with sin in a life and the harsh, accusatory, condemnatory spirit of spiritually superior, self-appointed judges. No person acting in the Spirit of Christ and the grace of God will "lay a guilt trip" on you, nor should you allow it to happen. Such treatment only intensifies the ailment. Jesus is the Great Physician. He will not break the bruised reed nor quench the smoking flax. Any truly Holy Spirit–directed ministry will flow in the power of God to do a healing work—not to inflict further pain. Guilt is part of the sickness; forgiveness is part of the cure. God's grace will pull you out of the slough of despond; man's condemnation will push you farther in.

Find the rock for your feet, and stand upon it. Learn to confess with the psalmist, "He brought me up also out of an horrible pit, out of the miry clay, and set my feet upon a rock, and established my goings. And he hath put a new song in my mouth, even praise unto our God: many shall see it, and fear, and shall trust in the LORD" (Psalm 40:2–3). Victory over the devil is an already-accomplished fact through the finished work of Christ. Learn to live in that victory as you learn to live in Him and celebrate the glorious reality that He also lives in *you*!

We come to Thee, our heavenly Father, as those who are captured
by Thy love. We adore Thee, we love Thee, we worship Thee.
Count us, O Lord, among the wise men who still seek Thee.
Heaven is the home of our spirits, and apart from Thy presence
we are as vagabonds. We have only one desire: to please Thee, for
not to please Thee is to be a disappointment to Thee, to ourselves,
and to everyone else. Thou hast given us life—only one life,
and we earnestly pray that by the power of Thy Spirit moving
within our hearts we may live it to Thy glory. In Jesus' name,
we pray. Amen.

Here Is Your Happiness

But if I, your teacher and Lord, have washed your feet,
you must be ready to wash one another's feet. . . . The
messenger is not greater than the man who sent him. Once
you have realized these things, you will find your happiness
in doing them" (John 13:14–17 PHILLIPS).

Jesus gave us an example to follow in our search for
happiness. Quite simply, it is in humbling ourselves and in
truly caring for one another in such a way that we will find
that an opportunity to serve is a rare privilege to be held
in esteem, as a gift from God's hand. The entire life of the
Lord Jesus teaches us this beautiful lesson. It is in bending
down that the spirit is ennobled, and through sacrifice that
the soul is enriched. It is in losing our rights that we gain
our privileges. The one desire of the humble spirit is to be
poured out, for he who saves his life will lose it, and he who

loses his life for Christ's sake shall find it.

Jesus began to tell us this as a baby in the manger in Bethlehem, having arrived in this world, not to profit by anything it had to offer, but to be poured out, and so we watch Him throughout His earthly life, giving, serving, loving, healing, caring, praying, teaching, blessing, and forgiving—and in the end, dying—all that He might by His life teach us how to live. And before He went away, He said, "I am going to leave something with you—a very special, precious gift: *My joy!*" Have you ever wondered about the kind of joy Jesus had? It was the kind of joy that comes with being poured out, a kind of joy of which the selfish are deprived. It doesn't come from being popular or rich or powerful; it comes from being reduced to love.

When we look at the baby Jesus lying in the arms of His mother, we see the very heart of God, the Father, *poured out*! When we see the holy, spotless Lamb of God, Jesus, our Savior, bleeding and dying on the cross, taking the place we, the sinners, deserved, we see the ultimate, supreme statement of humility, love, and sacrifice. And at the same time, we discover the secret of His joy. God, the Father, gave His Son in Bethlehem: Jesus gave Himself at Calvary.

Have you received the gift of His joy? It will be yours as you give yourself—to *Him*, and *to others*. As Jesus said, "Inasmuch as ye have done it unto one of the least of these my brethren, ye have done it unto me" (Matthew 25:40). Much giving: much joy. It's up to us!

We praise Thee, our Father, for the liberty of Spirit that was wrought for us through Christ's redeeming work. Thou hast set us free from the bondage of sin and loosed us from the chains of guilt. We praise Thee and worship Thee, and we rejoice in the fullness of our salvation. We gladly accept Thy lordship of our lives. Reign within our hearts and bring all things within us under the dominion of Christ, our Savior. This we pray in His holy name. Amen.

To Set the Captives Free

Jesus Christ came into the world to deliver captives and set at liberty those who are bruised. He came into the world bringing life, freedom, and love. He could do this for man because He is King of kings and Lord of lords, and when we give Him our allegiance, we are freed from bondage to other masters. We deny His lordship if we give ourselves over to the domination of any other. In our commitment to His authority, we are free—free to love and serve Him above and beyond all other relationships. We are free to respond to His love, free to obey His commands, free to express our worship to Him as the Holy Spirit teaches us to do.

This is one of the divine paradoxes: We are free to be captives; we are bound to Him by our love for Him, and loosed by Him by His love for us. By our commitment to His lordship, we are freed from the claims of the devil, for he has no right to touch that which belongs to God. Furthermore, we do not belong to other people. We belong to God, and to Him alone, by the sovereign act of His grace in having accepted us as His children and our having accepted His authority over our wills and over our lives.

We need to understand this basic spiritual law and, having understood, to be very careful to keep it in operation in our daily walk in the Spirit. If we are to walk in the light, it must be in the light of His Word. If His lordship is a reality in our everyday experience, we will have to be on guard at all times lest our own wills or the wills of others attempt to usurp the authority that by choice and by desire we have given to Christ.

We need protection against dominating spirits disguised as religious authorities who appoint themselves to be our spiritual guides, appearing to be holy but seeking for selfish reasons to control those within the circle of their influence. Professing to serve God, they are in fact serving themselves, consciously and unconsciously. A deluded person is right in his own eyes, unfortunately. They may well be among those who at the judgment say to Christ, "Have we not in your name done many mighty works?"—to whom He replies, "Depart from Me; I never knew you."

The individual with a dominating spirit is in need of insight to recognize the seriousness of moving in the direction of seeking power by control and seeking recognition in the adulation and approval of other people. When a dominating spirit is allowed free course and goes unchecked and unchallenged, it will draw about itself other spirits of pride, self-importance, superiority, and over-mastering. If, in turn, these expressions are excused, tolerated, and unchallenged, they will draw still other spirits, all of which are dangerous, destructive, anarchistic, and tyrannical. The more these spirits are fed, the stronger they become, and, in turn, all who have been victimized by the influence have less and less chance of escaping the net they have allowed to be drawn about themselves by having made their own contribution to the problem by giving subservience to the binding spirits of domination and supcriority.

We are slaves, the Bible tells us, to that which we allow. To willingly, thoughtlessly, or ignorantly put your soul under the influence of a dominating spirit is to jeopardize your own spirit and also to become responsible for a measure of the destructive results, having contributed to the making of a despotic personality.

"Follow me, for I am following Christ," said Paul. Every Christian should be able to say the same and should desire to have it so. To follow Christ is to walk in the same kind of humility He walked in. It is unthinkable that Jesus had a spirit of superiority. Everything about Him was the direct opposite. For He made Himself of no reputation, took the form of a servant, humbled Himself, and became obedient even to the death of the cross. He it is whom we worship, serve, honor, and adore, and if need be, for whom we would die. May we be protected and delivered from all false worship.

Jesus is Lord!

Almighty God, Thou who dost rule the universe by Thy divine omnipotence, grant, we pray, that we may find a way to express the depths of our gratitude for Thy mercy and Thy love. We bow at Thy feet; we bring our sins and ask forgiveness; we bring our brokenness and entreat Thee to grant us healing and renewed strength. The journey is long, and there is little to sustain us in the way. We look in vain for comfort from the world, but Thou hast not taught us to look to the world for comfort, and so we look to Thee, who hast never failed in the past and will not fail us now. We rejoice in all Thou art to us; we encourage our hearts in Thy greatness and marvel at Thy wonders, for we are daily witnesses to Thy never-failing watchfulness and Thy generous provision. We bless Thy name, O Lord, and vow anew our undying devotion to Thee. In Jesus' name, amen.

God of Hope and Patience

These two appellations come from Romans 15:13–14 and 15:5–6 as follows: "Now the *God of hope* fill you with all joy and peace in believing, that ye may abound in hope, through the power of the Holy Ghost. And I myself also am persuaded of you, my brethren, that ye also are full of goodness, filled with all knowledge, able also to admonish one anther." "Now the *God of patience* and consolation grant you to be likeminded one toward another according to Christ Jesus: that ye may with one mind and one mouth glorify God, even the Father of our Lord Jesus Christ."

To capture the underlying thought more directly, "May

the God of hope give you joy and peace as you trust in Him, and may you be full of goodness and understanding so that you may be a blessing to one another. And may the God of patience grant you harmony in Christ so that you may worship and glorify God the Father in unity of heart." This is not an improvement on the original text; it is simply a drawing together of the pertinent truths presented more directly to help us capture the intent. It is a prayer that believers may worship together in harmony. "Likeminded"—one mind, one mouth, one confession, that God may be glorified and all may be taught. Unity of expression comes from unity of mind. Oneness in mind comes from understanding and knowledge. *Instruction* in the Word is essential to purity in worship. "Filled with knowledge and able to admonish one another"—this can be true only if the mind has been schooled in the *Word*.

Much that passes for "worship" is no more than fleshly exercise. True worship is not generated by outward display. It is not a ritual to be entered into as part of a religious program. Group worship is glorifying God in unity of heart that has been developed in an atmosphere of patience and hope as the Word is bringing forth understanding and knowledge. God cannot be properly worshiped out of ignorance. One of the definitions of worship is "submissive respect," and this can be generated only by understanding. Faith is wonderful; but blind faith is nothing. Faith must be based on intelligent comprehension as to the kind of person we are trusting. To talk of faith and not understand the object is valueless.

Our faith is in a *person* whom we can understand only

as we are skilled in the *Word*, and we shall never be skilled in the Word until we take the time to *read* it! When we do that, we will find that, among other things (*many* other things!), God is a God of *hope* and a God of *patience*. Why do we need to understand this? Partly because we are so prone to be impatient pessimists. God is not like us, in our frailties. More to the point, He will never act in character according to our ignorance. He will always act according to His holiness and wisdom. This is why He is a continual disappointment to the carnal mind. The undisciplined, unsanctified nature of man demands God to perform in a fashion inconsistent with His character. If we understood Him as the God of hope and the God of patience, we would gain some insight, and little by little we might develop a measure of "submissive respect," and eventually perhaps we could learn something of how to enter into true *worship*. We would, hopefully, learn to approach the mercy seat with awe and wonder, with an appropriate attitude of humility—and with *patience* born of hope that springs from knowing that we are coming to a loving and wise heavenly Father who is truly listening and who desires to bless us, but who is above responding to petulance and most certainly cannot be moved or touched by tyranny.

Man will never force God to do anything. Never confuse *faith* with *force*. God is sovereign. God is supreme. God is loving. But He is to be honored, adored, obeyed, and loved—in patience and in hope, built on an intelligent understanding of His holy nature.

It is of Thy mercy, O Lord, that we are not consumed. Every morning we find our strength renewed and our courage fortified by the knowledge of Thy never-failing grace and rich supply. We are not cast upon our own limited resources, for we wholly cast ourselves upon Thee, even as Thou hast invited us to do. Surely Thou wilt be our strong support in every time of test and comfort in time of need. We praise, glorify, and magnify Thy name and ask Thee only that we never be guilty of ingratitude and never grieve Thy Spirit with complaint. Give us our own Song of Songs—a continuous melody of overflowing love in our hearts to Thee, to lift us above sadness and to encourage one another in the joy of the Lord. In Jesus' name, we pray, with thanksgiving. Amen.

God of Grace

One of the surest ways to encourage our hearts is filling our thoughts with the goodness and greatness of God. "Thou wilt keep him in perfect peace, whose mind is stayed on thee" (Isaiah 26:3). "My meditation of him shall be sweet; I will be glad in the LORD" (Psalm 104:34). "And David was greatly distressed; for the people spake of stoning him. . .but David encouraged himself in the LORD his God" (1 Samuel 30:6).

Whatever the situation in which we find ourselves, we will most speedily find relief as we set our thoughts on the Lord and praise Him for His mercies and tender love. I shall never live long enough to forget the impact on my heart of the poverty-stricken little children at the Westside Rescue Mission in Chicago as they heartily sang the little chorus "O, nothing really matters if the Lord loves me, and He does, oh yes, He does!" Another of their favorites was "Oh yes, my friend, there's something more, there's something more than gold; to know your sins are all forgiven is something more than gold."

Setting our minds on Him is more than a sentimental feeling. Concentrating on scriptures that give us insight into His character gives substance to our devotional intentions. The more we understand of the nature of God, the deeper will be our love for Him, for it is difficult to truly love anyone with whom we are not acquainted. The Bible is rich with revelation of God's personality, and as we search Him out through its sacred pages and meditate on the truths thus discovered, we will grow in our knowledge of Him and our love for Him will be enhanced.

With these thoughts in mind, let us consider 1 Peter 5:10, where we find Him referred to as the "God of all grace." 1 Peter 5:10–11 reads, "But the God of all grace, who hath called us unto his eternal glory by Christ Jesus, after that ye have suffered a while, make you perfect, stablish, strengthen, settle you. To him be glory and dominion for ever and ever. Amen." These beautiful verses follow a number of admonitions to (1) humble ourselves, (2) cast our cares on Him, and (3) be watchful for the devil and resist him steadfast in the faith. The theme of this particular letter of Peter's is suffering. Verse 10, above, mentions suffering. He most likely is referring not to physical pain but to spiritual affliction, as mentioned in

1 Peter 4:19: "Wherefore let them that suffer according to the will of God commit the keeping of their souls to him in well doing, as unto a faithful Creator."

There is little doubt that there is a close relation between some sort of spiritual affliction and growth in grace for the child of God, even as it is written of the Lord Jesus that He "learned. . .obedience by the things which he suffered" (Hebrews 5:8). We might like to entertain the idea that there may be some kind of suffering that does not inflict actual pain, but that is wishful thinking. Suffering is suffering, and suffering *hurts*. It hurt Jesus, and it will hurt us. It is the price of growth, of maturity, of perfection. It is partly in answer to prayer. Oh no, we do not pray for affliction, but when we pray for the perfecting action of the Spirit in our heats, the affliction will come in due course, as that is the instrument through which the perfecting work is accomplished. We speak sometimes of being "painfully aware" of certain things. That is part of the suffering in the spirit. The spotlight of divine conviction falls on some favorite sin or fault, and we wince with pain to realize that something we have harbored and nursed is indeed grievous to the heart of God, and we find ourselves relating to Peter when he "went out and wept bitterly." Beloved, that is suffering, and it hurts. And when you are laboring to do the will of God and all hell seemingly comes up against you to prevent the accomplishment of something that would bring a blessing to God's people, that is "suffering affliction."

There are probably as many ways to suffer in the spirit as there are ways to suffer in the flesh, and rest assured you will recognize it when it comes! And what are we to do with it? We are to offer it up to Him as a sweet-smelling sacrifice and *release it*. Never tense up when a pain hits. Don't fight it: Go with it. Let it have its way in you, and it will draw you into the heart of God, and it will turn to joy. That is what Jesus said when He concluded the Beatitudes with these words: "Blessed are ye, when men shall revile you, and persecute you, and shall say all manner of evil against you falsely, for my sake. Rejoice, and be exceeding glad: for great is your reward in heaven: for so persecuted they the prophets which were before you" (Matthew 5:11–12).

And while the suffering and affliction are going on, we are promised that we will be made perfect, stablished, strengthened, and settled. By whom? By the *God of grace*. Grace is one of the most beautiful and powerful attributes of the Godhead. Grace, we are told, is His divine favor extended to us in the face of our unworthiness. It is the hand of God reaching down in love, coming under our weakness and lifting us up into His arms of redemption. It was a glimpse of His grace that moved the songwriter to pen, "I will through the waves go singing, for one look at Him I love." Knowing His love for us, His mercy and His support, we can learn to endure with patience, being assured that "our light affliction, which is but for a moment, worketh for us a far more exceeding and eternal weight of glory" (2 Corinthians 4:17).

Yes, it is amazing grace, and it is *sustaining* grace. His grace will sweeten bitter waters, lift the burden of guilt, ease the load of heartache, and keep a song in the heart when the prospect is bleak. It is because of His grace that we can heartily proclaim with the psalmist, "The LORD is on my side; I will not fear: what can man do unto me?" (Psalm 118:6). And as Paul expressed it in Romans 8:31–32, "What shall we then say to these things? If God be for us, who can be against us? He that spared not his own Son, but delivered him up for us all, how shall he not with him also freely give us all things?"

Lean on His arm, dear friend; He will never fail. Rest in His love; He will rescue you from every snare. The government is on His shoulders; He will deal with the adversary. Trust His wisdom; He knows the way, and when He has tried us, we shall come forth as gold (Job 23:10). Praise His holy name! We need not falter, for truly *His grace is sufficient*. " 'Tis grace that brought us safe thus far, and grace will lead us home."

In Thee, O Lord, is our life and our strength. In Thy presence is fullness of joy. We would live this day in Thy presence, in the awareness that we are never out of Thy sight nor out of Thy mind, for as the psalmist wrote, "I am poor and needy; yet the Lord thinketh upon me" (Psalm 40:17). Surely Thy thoughts toward us are thoughts of deliverance and salvation. Thou art mindful of our weakness, but it is Thy desire to heal and to bless. You have commanded a blessing toward us, your children, and we look for good, not evil.* Accept our praise for your loving-kindness, heavenly Father, we pray. In Jesus' name, amen.

Christist Is Our Victory

God is able to strengthen His people by the indwelling power of Christ so that they shall be enabled to stand through whatever tests may come, knowing that in Him is their sufficiency, and from Him they can draw the necessary help, strength, and understanding.

God is daily confirming this truth as we see the manifestation of the inward work. There are always struggles, but there is also growing faith. Perfection is yet to come, but there is a pressing on and a striving for the goal. There are discouragements, there are doubts, but there is also a growing confidence and deepening consecration.

The seed planted is bearing fruit. The lives transformed are being daily strengthened in faith. God has not deserted

---

* See Deuteronomy 28:8, Psalm 42:8, Psalm 133:3—"the LORD *commanded* a blessing."

His people, and He never will. By His grace His people likewise will not desert Him! Some who are now going through valleys will be coming out into the sunshine in the days ahead; and some who are now in the sunshine may experience some valleys! But God is *faithful*, and our confidence is in Him. We do not put confidence in the flesh: Our confidence is in the Lord, that He is protecting and keeping and preserving those who are His, and that He will continue to do so.

It is human to waver and to experience days when discouragement moves in like a cloud and seemingly blots out the sunshine, but those days do not tell the story. They come and they go, but always faith is arriving on the scene again, like the sun rising in the morning, regardless of how many cloudy days may have passed. God has nowhere promised perfection in this life; but He has promised ultimate victory, and we claim that and press on. The end is always in view, victory is coming, and we can hold steady while He works everything out according to His purposes. We can encourage ourselves and each other in the Lord, for truly *He is our victory* and we rejoice in *Him*—not in ourselves. He is always in victory and in Him we are bound to win in the end, and the more we trust Him, the more often we will find ourselves in victory in the present moment. Bright hopes of the future by no means cancel the present needs. We have as much right to expect victory today as tomorrow. The secret is in resting in Jesus, standing still, and letting Him fight for us, as He has promised to do. If an action is needed on our part, we will get our guidance more clearly in the quietness of communion than in the "noisiness" of our feelings. Our biggest difficulty is in getting still. In the stillness, the answers come without pressure. The pressure usually comes from outward circumstances and other people's thoughts or actions. *HE IS OUR PEACE, HE IS OUR VICTORY, HE IS OUR COMFORT, HE IS ALL AND EVERYTHING. PRAISE HIS NAME!*

And all this is by the cross and by the shed blood. The blood has as much power to save us from our stresses as from our sins. It will do its healing work as we claim its power to break all the powers of darkness.

Loving heavenly Father, Thou who art the searcher of hearts, search our hearts, we pray, and deal with us according to Thy mercy; for we do not know our own needs. We want what is Thy best for us, but we do not know what that is. And so we come to Thee bringing our open hearts and kneeling at Thy feet in love and adoration. We bring our sins to be forgiven; we bring our hurts to be healed; we bring our ignorance to be enlightened. We worship Thee even as we pray that we may learn how truly to worship. We come as children to our Father, grateful that Thou dost understand our limitations, praising Thee for the sacrifice of Jesus for us and the precious gift of Thy Holy Spirit, our ever-present Counselor and Comforter. In Jesus' name, amen.

The Shell or the Seed?

God in His love and grace grants us from time to time some very precious experiences. Sooner or later, we find the scene has changed and what was is no more in the same form in which it had existed; but in the Spirit, nothing changes. The shell is gone, but the seed is still here. The outer has disappeared, but the inner remains. The flesh dies, but the Spirit lives.

Present and future progress is impeded when we hold on to that which has already passed away, clutching the empty shell when we ought to be scattering the living seed. The message is living. It is the message that we should press to our bosom—not the memory of past experiences, however inspiring they may have been. We need not cast away the inspiration of a past experience, but we must not dwell on the memory in retrospect and attempt to reconstruct some kind of replacement for that which is now gone. "Behold, I will do a new thing," says the Lord. The Spirit of God does not deal in repetitions. It is we who are prone to do this. God is the God of today and tomorrow. There is no place in the Spirit for nostalgia. We need memory healings of our yesterdays in order to gain health for today and strength for tomorrow.

God has great and wonderful things for those who dare to trust Him. Do not look for Him in the shadows of the past. He is not there. When they looked for Him in the tomb, He was not there. He was not wrapped in the grave clothes. They were empty! Beloved, you will never find Him by looking in the grave clothes of your past experiences. He is not there: Behold, He is alive, and He is going before you. He is always before you. Today is all we have. Yesterday is gone, and tomorrow is not yet here. We dare not live in the past nor try to reconstruct that which has already come to its own fulfillment. We each have to find our own vision and follow that. We are not called to perpetuate someone else's vision that has already come to completion. God has something wonderful for every one of His children, and it will be something new and something different. It will not be part of the shell but part of the seed; not of the flesh but of the Spirit; not of the personality but of Christ who frees every individual to be indeed an individual, bound only by his own personal commitment to the Lord Jesus Christ.

You may have bound yourself to the shell, but you were

never bound by the seed, for the seed is of the Spirit, and where the Spirit of the Lord is, there is liberty, there is freedom, and there is a continual unfolding of *new life*. We need to be delivered from whatever binds us to old patterns and our fascination with personalities. No individual who is truly in submission to the Spirit of Christ will desire to bind you to himself, nor would they desire that you be bound by someone else in their name. Beloved, we need a great loosening. He who is free in Christ and moving unbound in the Spirit will be at peace with his brothers and sisters in the Lord. What we seek and pray for individually, we must seek and pray for in order not to put bondages on one another, and that we all may be free to respond to the Holy Spirit.

God has not called us to do homage to a past ministry any more than He would ask us to mourn over a grave. We must forget the things that are behind and press toward the mark to gain the prize of whatever it is that God has in store for us now. We must cherish the living spirit of Christ which drew us together in the first place and which alone can sustain us now. We go through outward motions in worship, but the outward motions are not the reality. Christ, who is the object of our worship, is the reality. He has not left us. If every church in the world vanished tomorrow, He would still be here. We are not wishing the churches would vanish; we are only reaffirming the truth that Christ is bigger than all the buildings in the world, and His Spirit is the one reality—not human structures. We are not against the church; we are only stating that it is the living Christ within the church, and more precisely, within His people, who are the true church within the outer structure of the church that is the life force from which we draw our spiritual strength. If we feel put upon to preserve a structure even though the structure be not a building, we didn't get the message at all. We each have a divine commission we need to discover and fulfill. It is not to crawl back into somebody else's empty shell; it is to propagate the living seed of truth in whatever way God sees fit to do it through our yielded lives. Our commitment is to *Him*. It is not to a memory.

We are crowding the tape at the close of a race. Time is running out. Whatever we are going to do, we need to do speedily. Whatever is binding us in the area of personalities needs to be broken. If in any way we are binding others, may we be given insight to see this. If someone is clinging to me or to you, they need to be redirected to Christ lest their spiritual growth be hindered and we find ourselves responsible before God for feeding our self-love with the adulation of those whom we unwittingly encourage to follow us rather than to follow Him.

This is the message we may have heard a thousand times. We need to hear it continually repeated because we are so inclined to get entangled in personalities when we ought to be relating to Jesus with a singleness of heart that would spare us all the misery we bring upon ourselves in our weakness and stubbornness. The Spirit is indeed willing, but the flesh craves the false comfort of human support in spite of the fact that it is forever disappointing. If our eyes were opened, we would understand that God is trying to break our fascinations by those very disappointments; but we demand to have it our way and berate those who fail us.

God is waiting still, with outstretched arms and patient love, to gather us unto Himself and truly satisfy every longing of our hearts out of the fullness of His overflowing life. If we are hungry or thirsty or lacking in consolation, there is only one reason: We have not sought the warmth of His presence, and we have left His Word uneaten. The solution is an individual matter. Our victory is a private responsibility. Our joy will come from intimate fellowship with Jesus, or else we will be desolate. Jesus is the answer. He always has been, He always will be, and there will never be a different solution to our needs. It is this confidence that will hold the soul steady whatever comes—and whatever goes. We can help others by pointing the way, but the *way* is *Jesus*, and so we must ever point to *Him*, not to ourselves.

The Spirit of Christ is a ministering spirit of power blended with meekness and gentleness. This balance of faith and love, of strength and of gentleness, is essential to an effective witness. Free will is a sacred gift from God Himself and was an element of His divine image in which He created us. God never violates His own intention. He gave man free will, and man is responsible to make right choices; but God will never force man to make the right choice. He is not a despot. He will never act in such a way as to destroy His creation with His power. He woos man with His love, warns man with the knowledge of the rewards of evil, entices man with promises of blessings for the righteous, and then allows man to make his choice because He gave him that privilege and will not override it. The Spirit of Christ is in harmony with the love of God, and the love of God does not operate in the realm of coercion and force. It was the misguided disciples who said to Christ, "Wilt thou that we command fire to come down from heaven, and consume them [referring to Samaritans who did not welcome Jesus]?" (Luke 9:54). Jesus' reply was "No." It was Peter, not Jesus, who cut off the ear of the servant of the high priest. It was Jesus who restored it again with no consideration for the fact that these soldiers had come on an evil mission. The most effective way we can keep alive the true seed of the everlasting gospel is by shedding abroad the love and grace of God.

The Whistle

True spiritual ministry has nothing to do with personality, competition, or popularity. It has to do with preaching the Word, praying, and saving souls. The vessel used is like a whistle that God picks up and blows through for a time and then lays down. It is the Holy Spirit, not the whistle, that is the dynamic factor. We are favored if used, but humbled to know that at any time He may either pick up or set down. We can know that it is the Holy Spirit blowing through the whistle when the message exalts Christ, not the whistle.

*Our loving heavenly Father, as Thou hast shown mercy upon us,
let us also show mercy to others. As Thou hast extended to us Thy
love, may we in turn look upon our brothers with kindness and
compassion. Deliver us, O God, from a spirit of condemnation
that would add weight to another's burden. Grant us Thy peace
in our own hearts that we may bring that peace to those about
us and hasten the coming of Thy kingdom on earth. Let Thy love
rule our hearts. For Jesus' sake, amen.*

Humility, the Grace of the Self-Divested

Many there are who boast great things in their religious
zeal. Thinking themselves to be wise, they become fools in
their spiritual pride, setting themselves up as examples of
purity, judging their brothers with lofty arrogance, forgetting
that it is by the grace of God, and only by the grace of
God, that any soul is justified in the eyes of the Father. The
chastened soul will confess with sincerity that he is chief
of sinners and unworthy to be called even a servant of the
Lord. He will look upon his brother with charity and upon
the erring with forgiveness. Charity, we read, is not puffed
up, is easily entreated, and views the actions of others in the
best possible light. It is not in the nature of humility to pass
judgment on the sinner and wield the rod of correction in a
spirit of vindictiveness.

Humility is not to be equated with slaves: It is the glory
of kings. "The God of Israel said. . .He that ruleth over men
must be just, ruling in the fear of God. And he shall be as the

light of the morning, when the sun riseth, even a morning without clouds; as the tender grass springing out of the earth by clear shining after rain" (2 Samuel 23:3–4).

Kindness is never to be divorced from justice, but with a spirit of meekness we are instructed to restore a man taken in a fault, considering the fact that we also are in danger of being tempted (Galatians 6:1). Gentleness is one of the fruits borne of the Spirit (Galatians 5:22), and as such it is to be cultivated and evidenced in our patience with our fellow believers as we all go through many varied experiences both in victories and defeats and are trained by the Spirit in the gentle ways of Jesus, who did not break the bruised reed.

How grateful we are for His unending patience with us! How many times we have failed Him! How often we have turned to our own ways and missed His best and highest! Lamentations 3:22 reads, "It is of the LORD's mercies that we are not consumed, because his compassions fail not." How we need to exercise that kind of compassion toward our brothers lest they be consumed by our condemnation of them.

Habakkuk prayed, "O LORD. . .in wrath remember mercy" (Habakkuk 3:2). It was a prayer for revival. Let us also pray for revival—for a renewing of our first love and a quickening of our languishing spirits and a refreshing of our souls. And in our battle against sin and the Destroyer, *let us remember mercy!*

Heavenly Father, we look to Thee this day for Thy sustaining grace, for strength to meet the challenges, for Thy peace to garrison our hearts and Thy love to preserve our spirits. There is little in the world to charm, but having Thee, what need we more? Though it may seem that we journey alone, in truth it is not so, for Thy companionship surpasses all other. Bless, we pray, all who are in special need of Thy healing and comforting touch. Deliver those in bondage, and bring understanding to those in confusion. Grant a measure of peace, we pray, in our world, and especially within our own hearts, that we may be Thy messengers of hope in a world of doubt and uncertainty. Let Thy Spirit rest upon us. In Jesus' name, we pray. Amen.

Victory Is Secured

Let the devil do his worst: God has done His best. "I've seen the lightning flashing, and heard the thunder roll. I've felt sin's breakers dashing, trying to conquer my soul. I've heard the voice of my Savior, telling me still to fight on. He promised never to leave me, never to leave me alone."

Praise God, we may not feel strong in ourselves, and indeed, we are not; but we have Someone dwelling within us who has conquered every foe, and He is still conquering.

Many are the dangers through which we pass each day—some known, others unknown, but God is the Keeper of our soul. Many are the questions to which we may have found no answers, but the One who understands all things stands beside us, and we shall not lose our way as we walk in Him, for He is the Way. He is not *a* way: He is *the* Way. To be centered in Christ is to be centered in truth even while we have yet much to learn. Understanding is a slow and painful process; but we are saved not by *knowledge* but by *faith*. While we are searching for wisdom, we can *abide* in simple trust, and God in some incomprehensible way will effect His divine purposes in spite of our ignorance.

We need not be unduly burdened about our inadequacies. "There is a place of quiet rest, near to the heart of God." He knows our frame and remembers that we are dust. It is because we are needy that He proffers His help. It is because we have failed that He extends His forgiveness. It is because of our poverty that He makes available to us His riches. "Blessed are the poor in spirit: for theirs is the kingdom of heaven" (Matthew 5:3). To be at ease in the presence of God requires an unburdening of the soul of preconceived notions concerning our own worthiness. We must settle it once and for all that we do not have, and never will have, anything within ourselves to commend ourselves to His majestic deity. This is not a bafflement to God. The consternation is on our part, in that we find it difficult to truly comprehend His amazing grace.

To lose sight of the efficacy of the redemptive work of the Lord Jesus Christ is to be cast upon a false system of rewards and punishment fabricated from our humanistic instincts. The gospel message of good news is that Christ died for our sins. It is that simple. And it is that profound! We can add nothing. And if we take something away, we have manufactured another gospel that is not the true gospel. Every false religion has done precisely this. Not being content to accept the fact that we are all sinners for whom Christ has died, other elements more acceptable to the innate pride of human nature have been substituted in place of the truth. Having opted for this replacement of fact with fable, the deluded religionist finds solace in resting in a place of spiritual pride, quite apart from a vital relationship with God that can be established and sustained only through the blood atonement of the Lord Jesus Christ.

There is no one who has provided peace with God for man through a sacrificial death other than Jesus. He, and He alone, is the Lamb of God, slain from the foundation of the world. Any other system of "salvation" by either good works or superior wisdom is a system of man's own making, not of God's, and it is well to remember that while we may deceive ourselves in thinking that we can make our own rules in this life, it is *He* who guards the gate of heaven. Those who are enticed into following the religions of man will discover to their own undoing the error when the day arrives that all things are revealed.

Yes, there is victory through Christ, for in Him, and in Him alone, is our peace, forgiveness, life, and hope. He has not left us orphaned. He has sent His Holy Spirit, the blessed Comforter, and has made us joint heirs of His riches in glory. Praise His name!

Our Lord and our God, it is with joy that we come to Thee, for Thou hast been faithful to us in every time of need. Thou hast showered upon us Thy bountiful goodness and upheld us with Thy righteousness. We have never sought Thee and been disappointed. We have never called that Thou hast not heard. We bless Thee, we magnify Thy name, we honor Thee and adore Thee. Grant that we may never neglect to offer Thee a full measure of gratitude and that we may never dishonor Thy name. May Christ be lifted up that all may be drawn unto Him, in whose name we pray. Amen.

The Realities of the Spirit

It is by the power of His indwelling Holy Spirit that we are sustained. It is by His precious Word that we are nourished. It is by His hand that we are led. Pilgrims and sojourners in a strange land, looking for that city that hath foundations, whose builder and maker is God, we travel on by faith. Not desiring to turn back, we seek a better country, and a city that God has prepared for us (Hebrews 11). The true child of God lives and moves in a sphere separate and apart from the worldly plane. He is in the world but not of the world; for he has been born again, not of corruptible seed, but of incorruptible, and he has a heavenly heritage. He has the mind of Christ; and while giving proper attention to the responsibilities of this life, he does not allow himself to become entangled with its affairs, that he may please Him who has chosen him to be a soldier of Jesus Christ (2 Timothy 2:4).

When the day comes that we stand before Him and the wood, hay, and stubble are burned in the fire—when only the gold, silver, and precious stones abide—in that hour it will be made manifest where we have laid up our treasure. Consecration and dedication have their reward, but not necessarily in this life. Bear patiently, then, each day's load of care. Look not on the outward, but *look up*! For our rewards are eternal rewards, and we go each step in the strength He provides.

This is no escapist message, for the things that are seen were not made of things that do appear (Hebrews 11:3). The realities of the Spirit are of more substance than the materialism of this world. The unregenerate man finds himself adrift in a sea of uncertainty and insecurity because everything in the world, said the wisest man, is "vanity"— emptiness. Only the mind that is stayed on Christ is a mind that can know perfect peace (Isaiah 26:3). Praise God! Praise Him in all things—the things that look good and the things that look bad—for He makes all things work together for the fulfilling of His purposes. The soul who is resting in Him will be content for the "all things" to work *for God's purposes* rather than for his own selfish purposes.

> *He knows, He loves, He cares,*
> *Nothing this truth can dim.*
> *He gives His very best to those*
> *Who leave the choice with Him.*
> —Anonymous

God is neither blind to our needs nor deaf to our cries. He is an ever-present help in time of need, and it is not surprising that those who have come to know Him the most intimately and to love Him the most deeply are those who have had the most frequent and the direst experiences of desperation. Therefore, we ought most sincerely to be truly grateful for every trial and to praise Him in the place of difficulty, and not to wait to praise Him until *after* the victory has come. It was while Paul and Silas were still in prison, beaten and bloody, at the midnight hour, that they sang praises; and Jesus joined in the singing, for where two or three are gathered in His name, there is He in the midst. It is unlikely that we will ever find ourselves in a worse condition; but in every situation, however deplorable, to continue to love Him and praise Him is the key to certain victory.

O weary soul, do not despair.
Cast now on Him thine every care.
Lay at His feet thy heavy load;
He walks with thee the lonely road.
Be not afraid, for in His love,
Angels attend thee from above.
However dark may be the night,
Christ is thy guide and Christ thy light.

Never give up, for the battle is the Lord's, but the victory is ours. The psalmist David said, "O God the Lord, the strength of my salvation, *thou hast covered my head in the day of battle*" (Psalm 140:7). Surely we can know the same protection. It matters not how sharp the conflict nor how the arrows fly. The God of our salvation will protect us: He will cover our head. Praise His holy name! We go from day to day in the strength of the Lord, and it is He, and He alone, who preserves the soul, and we overcome the enemy by the blood of the Lamb and by our word of testimony.

Prayer and praise bring the help of God to the suffering saint. We have a great High Priest who is touched with our feeling of infirmities, for He was tempted in all points like as we are, yet without sin. Let us therefore come boldly unto the throne of grace, that we may obtain mercy and find grace to help in time of need. Out of much suffering the soul is made pure. Through much conflict the spirit is made strong. God holds within His hand the fabric of our lives and fashions as He pleases. We shall one day see clearly that which He has wrought. Our confidence and trust in Him bring harmony between what He is doing in us and what we are desiring to do to please Him. We may fall far afield of our highest goals in this life, but if our ultimate goal is God Himself, we shall not be disappointed, for there is no disappointment in Him.

"Now the God of peace, that brought again from the dead our Lord Jesus, that great shepherd of the sheep, through the blood of the everlasting covenant, make you perfect in every good work to do his will, working in you that which is wellpleasing in his sight, through Jesus Christ; to whom be glory for ever and ever. Amen" (Hebrews 13:20–21).

Heavenly Father, move upon our hearts by the power of Thy Holy Spirit and bring us into full surrender to Thy will. Teach us what it is to be totally submissive to Thee, loving Thee for what Thou art, asking nothing but to have the privilege to worship and serve Thee all the days of our lives. Grant Thy forgiveness for all our sins, and give us grace to walk in paths of righteousness. For Jesus' sake, we pray. Amen.

Rebellion, Witchcraft, and False Prophets

This may be a startling message, but we are living in a day when we need to be awake and alert. Human nature has a tendency to block out whatever threatens to be disturbing to our consciousness. Any consequent sense of security is false. Realities do not vanish because we choose to dismiss them from our minds. Another device we use to put the unpleasant out of our recognition is to assign it to archaic times, but there is nothing obsolete about witchcraft. It is very much with us today, and yet we are for the most part startled if we are in any way brought into a confrontation with it. It is not wisdom to choose to ignore danger in any form. "Forewarned is forearmed" is applicable in this regard. We can be informed without being alarmists. Fear is not an answer: It is one more problem. This is not presented to instill fear as to demonic powers, but rather to present basic information for the protection of God's people, for "knowledge is power."

What we understand to be evil, we will avoid unless we are walking in rebellion, and this is the subtle tie between the two. "Rebellion," the Bible says, "is as the sin of witchcraft" (1 Samuel 15:23). The heart that harbors rebellion is an open channel for the entrance of evil powers, for it has not the protection of God's blessing. The heart that cries, "Jesus is Lord," can be moved upon by the Spirit of God. The Spirit of rebellion refuses to confess the lordship of Christ and will not submit to His rule. To heartily confess that "Jesus is Lord" is more than repeating a nice-sounding slogan. It is the difference between submission and rebellion—the difference between the power of the Holy Spirit ruling a life or the powers of evil moving in and taking over. And we should not console ourselves that there may be some relatively safe area in between. Don't risk it! Those who have done so will be first to sound the warning!

There are those who are operating in the area of demonic powers who are doing so under the false pretense of being religious teachers. Jesus said we could distinguish the true from the false by their fruits. Part of the "fruit" is the method of operation. Jesus *chose* disciples, but there was no *force* involved. There was no *pressure* in their calling and no compulsion exerted to hold them captive. They were free to choose to follow, and they were free to leave, as Judas did.

And although following Jesus meant giving Him priority, it did *not* mean parental repudiation. "Honor thy father and thy mother" was the command of Jesus, recorded in three Gospels—Matthew, Mark, and Luke—and reemphasized by the writer of Ephesians (see 6:2). Also see Deuteronomy

5:16. Breaking family ties—particularly children from parents in the guise of Christian commitment—is a red light flashing to warn you that something is amiss. There is no indication in the Bible that parents have to be ostracized from their children in order for the children to follow Jesus. Indeed, if Christ taught that we should honor our father and our mother, how can we please Him by doing otherwise, and how can we honor our parents and ostracize them both at the same time?

There is one thing you will always find true about Jesus: He was always consistent, and none of the teachings of Jesus ever conflict with His commandments. It is flattering to the ego to feel that we have "progressed"—that we are living in the Spirit and free from the bondage of the law. The truth is that if we are walking in the Spirit, we will never "progress" to a place where God's commandments do not apply. Beware of people who have, by their own standards, become so spiritual that they are beyond the reach of the laws of God. It is true that this is the age of grace, but it is also true that the Bible says His Word will endure forever, and Jesus said, "If a man love me, he will keep my words" (John 14:23), and His commandments were basically the same as those that were delivered by the angel of the Lord to Moses. (1) Love God, worship only Him, put Him first, make Him Lord. (2) Treat your brother right—love him and be kind. (3) Honor your parents. There were ten, not three, but these are basic, and they have not been changed. Jesus gave many more, but none that conflicted with these.

We are saved by grace through faith, not by self-effort,

for it is the gift of God, not of works lest we be tempted to boast. But the Word also tells us in Romans 8:4 that those who are walking in the Spirit will fulfill (live in harmony with) the laws of God (not in conflict with or in opposition to the basic commandments of God). This is not "legalism"; this is an outward manifestation of an inward work of God's saving grace in the heart. The new concept that Jesus taught was that by the work of the indwelling Holy Spirit in the heart of the believer, a man can be so regenerated and empowered that he can express a behavior pattern in harmony with all the biblical commandments. To believe, on the contrary, that the new birth or any religious experience is a royal road to rebellion is as false a concept as any heresy can ever be. Yes, there is freedom and liberty in the Spirit—but it is freedom from *sin* and liberty to serve and obey Christ: It is *not* freedom to express self-will.

Our Lord and Father, we come to Thee in gratitude and worship. Thou hast showered upon us Thy blessings until there is no room to receive. Thou hast poured out upon us Thy love and Thy kindness until we are overwhelmed with Thy greatness. Give us the will to share with others with the same free abandonment with which Thou hast blessed us. May we ever be mindful of those less fortunate, remembering that Thou hast said that like as we have done unto others, so have we done unto Thee. Forgive us our sins both of omission and of commission, and teach us to walk in the power of Thy Holy Spirit. In Jesus' name, we pray. Amen.

The Lordship of Christ

The person who continues in a spirit of selfishness and rebellion will go to hell no matter how many churches he may belong to or how many Bibles he carries. Why? Because being born again and a true believer carries with it a commitment to Christ that implies that He be enthroned in the heart as King, Ruler, Lord, Master—the One whose wishes and commands will be respected and obeyed. This is what it means to love and serve Him. It means *obedience* and *submission* to His will.

It is so easy to verbalize these things; but when it comes down to the reality of putting them into practice, some act as though they had never been exposed to the concept, going merrily on their way, doing precisely as they wish, pleasing themselves at any cost, catering to their whims and personal desires, and acting for all intents and purposes as though they had never heard of the lordship of Christ. Beloved, if the lordship of Christ is something that you are only verbalizing and not experiencing, you had better go back to the beginning and reexamine your relationship to Him and find out whether you are actually born again and a child of God or just a professing Christian with no real life at all—no true spiritual nature born of the Spirit. *Something* should be manifesting in terms of likeness to Jesus, who was submissive to His Father's will.

Free, full, and complete submission to the lordship of Christ is the best protection we can ever have against dark forces and demonic influences. We need to be reminded that such powers of evil do not necessarily appear as such when they initially present themselves to us. The channel of approach may be through a treasured and delightful friend or relative—or a preacher. Deception is one of the prime tools of the enemy. The devil will make following Jesus seem very drab in comparison to the colorful enticements of the occult world. Fortune-telling, astrological charts, and such things capture the spirit of curiosity in human nature and are another channel of operation for demonic influences. All of these things are strictly forbidden in scripture, and God has warned of their destructive effects on the soul. Dabbling in the occult in any form will interfere with the influence of the Holy Spirit in the life of a believer. It is either Christ or Satan. It cannot be both. There is no room for compromise. There is no such thing as having a bit of each. We are either a child of God or a child of the devil. We are either in submission to Christ or in submission to Satan.

This is the point where rebellion, either conscious or subconscious, must be recognized as the most dangerous of all the sins of the spirit. Outer sins that are so much talked about and condemned are like snowflakes in comparison to the iceberg of rebellion. The most alarming thing is that many a person who has rid himself of the snowflakes is still in the death grip of the iceberg. Hell will be peopled not so much with alcoholics and prostitutes as with the *rebellious*, untold thousands of whom are on the church membership rolls, have been duly baptized, and have paid their tithes. People like these were responsible for the crucifixion of Jesus. They were professedly religious but inwardly rebellious! They loved religion, but they inwardly hated God. They resented interference from a higher power that opposed their self-will. Beloved, Christianity is no child's play or sweet, gentle sentiment.

If you are waiting for God to bless your rebellion, you will wait in vain. God is not obligated to respond to your demands. He is not deaf to your clamoring. He is simply impervious to violent assault. He is waiting for you to approach Him in the humility of spirit that is the only appropriate attitude for a sinner to assume. He will not be intimidated or manipulated to respond to your demands. This may be your modus operandi with other people, but it will not work with God. He is sovereign, holy, just, and equitable, but He is not maneuverable. When He is approached in love and adoration and humbleness, He will not withhold any good thing. He extends His mercy to the poor in spirit, but the "rich" He sends away empty. It is our sins that separate us from Him, and our rebellion brings us into poverty. Righteousness will bring His blessing, but a selfish spirit will bar the gate of heaven and cut off the stream of divine mercy.

We pray, O God, this day for the wisdom to discern between good and evil and for the will to choose only the good. We are beset round about with evil forces. Protect us by Thy Spirit, but grant us also the understanding not to walk in a slippery path. Guard us and guide us in the way of holiness that we may be spared the ravages of sin and may teach others to do likewise. This we pray for all Thy children everywhere. In the name of Christ, our Lord, amen.

God Is Not Mocked

Be not deceived; God is not mocked, whatever we sow, that shall we reap. It is the nature of God to love, but He cannot extend His love in the face of rebellion. He will not tolerate impudence. You may succeed in manipulating a few permissive friends, but you will never manipulate God. He is not your servant: He is your *Master*. You may dominate people, but you will not dominate Him. If you are a born-again Christian and are still ruled by a demanding, rebellious spirit, you are carnal, not spiritual; and "to be carnally minded," the Bible tells us, "is death; but to be spiritually minded is life and peace" (Romans 8:6). The heart of the "spiritual" man is filled with peace, love, and joy. The "carnal" soul is filled with unrest, guilt, fear, and hate. You can judge your own self. Into which category do you fall? Being religious counts for nothing. The Pharisees were religious. The hypocrites were religious. No one who is "in the Spirit" is full of resentment and frustration. God is *love*, and His Spirit is a spirit of love and peace, gentleness and forgiveness, mercy and grace. "If we would judge ourselves, we should not be judged" (1 Corinthians 11:31).

Religious cults and communes that capture our young people and alienate them from their homes draw their power to influence and control the unsuspecting from the areas of rebellion in their spirits. That is one point of vulnerability. The other open door that presents an invitation into enslavement is the need for love and acceptance that has its roots in self-rejection. Such an individual will accept an offer of what appears to be social warmth and togetherness and not count the cost in terms of loss of personal freedom. When the enslavement progresses from body to soul and ultimately to spirit, the damage is often beyond repair, and the end is a pit of all sorts of abusive and perverse behavior patterns. The trap of deception snaps shut on the victim, and he is not only powerless to escape but willing to remain in his helpless condition, for he has given over control of his will to powers beyond himself.

Parents, pay attention to what your young children, including your preschoolers, are watching on television. The presentation of witchcraft on children's programs is becoming increasingly commonplace. Séances, witches dancing around fires, etc., are cleverly slipped into what might otherwise be considered harmless children's programs, and your children are being conditioned to think such things as being normal and acceptable. You may think it does no harm because they don't understand what they are viewing, but the images are indelibly etched on the mind, consciously or unconsciously, and the damage is being done of opening channels of access for demonic influences by this exposure to the occult world. Many a Christian parent who insists on their children having their education through Christian schools are permitting their children to see things by way of television that are far more dangerous than public school. Mother, while you are washing dishes in the kitchen, the devil is brainwashing your little children in the living room in front of the television set, and you will ultimately pay dearly for the "free babysitter" in terms of evil influences that are laying hold on your children's minds. It is far easier to prevent damage than to correct it. Beloved, witchcraft and demonism are *not* acceptable, and as part of an entertainment program, this sort of thing will prove itself to be incredibly costly in the price it exacts in terms of spiritual damage. It is a price we can't afford to pay, for eternal souls are in the balance.

We have not herein discussed deliverance ministry. A wealth of material is available on the subject. The purpose of what has been written is to sound a warning. Christ is greater than Satan. There is power in the name of Jesus and power in His shed blood for deliverance. But until we are through with self-will and rebellion, we will be needing a deliverance prayer every day of the week. There are ways to get out of trouble, but how much better to keep out of trouble in the first place. If your house is burning, you can call the firemen, but a smoke detector might have prevented the fire. Christ is able to deliver us out of all our troubles, but an ounce of prevention is still worth a pound of cure, and our safeguard against evil lies in establishing and maintaining a vital, close relationship with Christ, abiding in Him in humble submission and ardent devotion, praying without ceasing, praising from a grateful heart, loving to do His will, and delighting in His law. His law and love and His will and grace are go-togethers. You have to accept both sides of the coin. You'll never get His love without His law nor His grace without His will. He doesn't have two sets of rules—one for the obedient and another for the disobedient. There is no provision in His grace for the disobedient. "Rebellion is as the sin of witchcraft" because rebellion is of the devil and rebellion will put you in the devil's camp as surely as murder. It can be hidden under self-righteousness; it can be concealed under "good works"; it can be disguised under a cloak of religiosity; but it is a deadly force and will sooner or later surface and destroy everything good in its path.

Our Father, we need Thy constant care and protection. We know Thou art greater than all the power of the enemy. We take the believer's authority over all dark forces and every destructive thing that would come against our souls to work evil. We look to Thee for our deliverance through the blood of Jesus and the power of His name. We thank Thee for victory through Christ, our Lord. Amen.

The Full Armor

The Old Testament is a history of God's patience and man's rebellion, and this gloomy story was prefaced by Lucifer's rebellion in heaven prior to the Genesis creation. Rebellion is nothing new. It is the age-old expression of all that is evil resisting all that is good. Until it is eradicated from our hearts, we will never experience the victory Christ died to give us. Deliverance ministries would not be necessary if every believer would allow the Spirit of Christ to do a continuous work of crucifying the old carnal nature within each of us, which if allowed to live will bring us continual defeat. Demons wait to enter whenever self-will cracks the door. The devil is no respecter of persons. The fact that you are respectable, successful, intelligent, or cultured gives you no protection. He may even have a preference for such! No, our protection is in abiding under the shadow of the Almighty and hiding under the shelter of His wings, for He alone has ultimate power and authority over the powers of darkness and forces of evil.

May the Holy Spirit apply the truth to our hearts, bring us into submission to the Spirit of Christ, establish our lives in divine order, and fill us with all joy and peace in believing. May we walk worthy of Christ, in whom is no darkness. May we be delivered of all malice and hate and resentment that we may receive His forgiveness and His love and express the same to others. "For our conversation is in heaven; from whence also we look for the Saviour, the Lord Jesus Christ: who shall change our vile body, that it may be fashioned like unto his glorious body, according to the working whereby he is able even to subdue all things unto himself" (Philippians 3:20–21). "Christ also suffered for us, leaving us an example, that ye should follow his steps: who did no sin. . .who his own self bare our sins in his own body on the tree, that we, being dead to sins, should live unto righteousness: by whose stripes ye were healed. For ye were as sheep going astray; but are now returned unto the Shepherd and Bishop of your souls" (1 Peter 2:21–22, 24–25).

Finally, "The peace of God, which passeth all understanding, shall keep your hearts and minds through Christ Jesus" (Philippians 4:7). And from Colossians: "That ye might be filled with the knowledge of his will. . .that ye might walk worthy of the Lord. . .being fruitful in every good work. . .strengthened with all might, according to his glorious power. . .giving thanks unto the Father, which hath made us meet to be partakers of the inheritance of the saints in light: who hath delivered us from the power of darkness, and hath translated us into the kingdom of his dear Son: in whom we have redemption through his blood, even the forgiveness of sins" (1:9–14).

This message is the outgrowth of many experiences in observing the strategies of the enemy in his attempt to harass, confuse, and destroy the saints of God. The full armor of God is provided for us, but it is we ourselves who are instructed to "put it on." If we fail to put it on, we cannot expect to resist and survive the attacks of the evil one, who is still untiringly going about as a roaring lion, "seeking whom he may devour" (1 Peter 5:8). We must resist him for ourselves, and we must resist him on behalf of our brothers and sisters in Christ. Our warfare is not against each other: Our battle is against the enemy of our souls, and we need to stand against his destructive attacks individually and collectively.

May we seek His face as never before in intercessory prayer for the entire body of Christ, that the power of God may prevail over the powers of darkness in every true child of God. It is the meaning of the very words Christ taught us to pray: "Thy kingdom come. Thy will be done in earth, as it is in heaven." May His kingdom (rule and authority) be set up in our hearts and His will be our sincerest desire, and it may be that we shall begin to experience a small foretaste of heaven on earth!

*Heavenly Father, our hearts overflow with praise and gratitude
to Thee for the never-failing bounty of Thy grace and mercy
that have been extended to us, Thy children. For the unmerited
gift of Thy love and forgiveness, we give Thee thanks. From
hearts that have been fed by Thy Word and healed by the power
of Thy Holy Spirit, we offer Thee praise. Accept this, our gift to
Thee, we pray, in the matchless name of Christ, our Savior and
Lord. Amen.*

Heirs of God

Our gift of gratitude we would lay at the feet of our
Lord, knowing full well how unworthy we are of all His
many blessings. Our sins have separated us from Him, but
His grace and forgiveness have brought us near. We rejoice
in the reconciling power of the atoning work of Christ, as
we claim by faith our oneness in Him who is our eternal
abiding place. In Him we are new creatures, and we claim
our new nature even as we renounce the old. For we are
children of grace, born into the family of God to walk in
the light of His Spirit. We are no longer any part of the
darkness. We are no longer slaves to the sin nature. We
rise up in faith and lay hold on our inheritance, for we are
heirs of God and joint heirs with Christ (Romans 8:17).
All He has willed for us is at our disposal. It is our privilege
to enjoy all that is of the divine nature to the extent of our
determination to do so, for He will grant us the desires
of our hearts. No power in heaven, on earth, or in hell

can separate us from His love and grace. Praise His name forever! It is not an idle tale nor an empty dream. The love of God toward His trusting children will endure when all else has failed. It will redeem, restore, and revive. It will bring order out of chaos, peace out of strife, and beauty out of ashes. It is a crown of glory on the heads of the saints, and to those who mourn it is balm from Gilead.

Yes, we are indeed grateful, and in our gratitude we would not be unmindful of those less fortunate who have not yet tasted of the water of life and have not been partakers of the heavenly feast. May we spread the good news of salvation and extend God's love to the hungry who cross our paths. May we be ambassadors of glad tidings, letting the light of God's Word shine into the darkness of the world around us, for truly the time is short, the days are evil, and we have no promise of tomorrow. And for this reason we have been given the power of His Holy Spirit, that we might be witnesses unto Him to our families, in our own country, and to the ends of the earth.

We praise Thee, our Father, for every blessing bestowed by Thy hand. We are grateful for life and strength and for the desire Thou hast placed in our hearts to love Thee and to serve Thee. Grant us grace to this end: that our energies may be spent for the good of others and for the glory of God. Deliver us from a selfish spirit that would hinder our usefulness and from every inclination to serve ourselves or to avoid the sacrifices in line of duty. We anticipate the soon return of the Lord Jesus Christ and pray for Thy perfecting work to be accomplished in us in preparation for that glorious day. In His name, we pray. Amen.

Back to Basics

"The heart is deceitful above all things, and desperately wicked," wrote the prophet Jeremiah (Jeremiah 17:9). And the apostle Paul wrote in Romans 7:18, "I know that in me (that is, in my flesh,) dwelleth no good thing." And in Romans 3:23, "All have sinned, and come short of the glory of God."

This is the starting point. This is the reason for Calvary. This is the condition in which we came into this world. This we inherited from Adam. This is our fleshly, carnal, rebellious nature. This is the Bible doctrine of the "total depravity of man," and if it disturbs you, you do not have a foundation of fundamental truth but a "bootstrap" religion of humanistic origin. Jesus never taught that human nature was good in any way, shape, or form, and if He had been born of an earthly father, He could not have been the sinless sacrifice for us.

Bootstrap religion says that man can work his way into heaven by self-improvement and through religious practice. There are an endless variety of groups that operate on this principle, a majority of which we are quick to identify. The more alarming thing is that this type of thinking is becoming so widespread that unless we are alert, its seeds will be sown and take root in the very midst of historic, Bible-believing churches. If an evil is labeled, we will, hopefully, shun it. It is the insidious thoughts that creep in when we are unsuspecting that catch us off guard and permeate our thinking before we realize what has happened.

Humanism says, "Every man has a 'spark of the divine' in them that only needs to be fanned to bring it to life, and given time and opportunity, he will prove his worth. We should always think only the best of ourselves and all others, for are we not all performing to the best of our ability? And if it may not appear that way, there is a perfectly valid reason due to limitations of circumstances. Be patient, be tolerant, for regardless of apparent shortcomings, we are all in this together, and who is to say that anyone is better than another, for we are all a mixture of 'positives and negatives' and God is love. Let us 'live in the house by the side of the road, and be a friend to man.' I am *okay*, and you are *okay*. Everybody's beautiful. All's well with the world, and heaven is waiting to welcome us."

Does that sound familiar? We hear it on every hand, in one form or another, but, beloved, it is not Bible theology. I am *not okay*, and you are *not okay*. We are sinners.

We are rebels, and we are bent toward evil. We have a natural capacity for the vilest of crimes. Even our "best righteousnesses," the Bible says, are as "filthy rags" in the sight of God. This is the problem that Jesus shed His blood to solve. This is why we need a new birth—because we were born under the curse of sin. We need to be regenerated because we were born degenerate. The gospel message is not an invitation for all good men to enter the family of God because He is in need of our service. This we could do with no loss of face; but that is not the way it is. God is in no way in need of the services of depraved men and women, which we all are. It is we who are in need of the redeeming work of Christ in our hearts through the power of His shed blood, to rescue us from eternal damnation and take us out of the kingdom of darkness and translate us into the kingdom of His dear Son. We who have no righteousness of our own are in need of the righteousness of Christ to be put to our account through faith in His finished work of salvation on our behalf. Becoming a Christian is not like joining a club. The church is not a gathering of morally elite, genteel people. It is the company of saints who have become saints by being washed in the blood of the Lamb and by repudiating the old sinful nature, having been born anew in holiness through repentance and faith.

This is not humanism. This is diametrically the opposite. Humanism is nowhere to be found in the Bible. Humanism is a contrivance of man to salvage his pride and ego. It is a philosophical fire-escape from hell, erected by man to save man. Beloved, man will never save man. Religion will never save man. Man is doomed. We must have divine intervention, and this is why we need Jesus, who was not only a man but God the Son, with power in Himself to overcome sin, and power through the atonement to deliver us also from the penalty, the power, and ultimately the presence of sin. This is Christianity, and it bears no semblance to humanism. It is written that Jesus did not come into the world to condemn the world but to save. That is true, because the sentence of condemnation had already been passed and man was *already* condemned; so the good news of the gospel is that man, who is already under the sentence of death because of his sins, can pass out from under condemnation by putting his faith in Christ, and can pass from death (the state in which he was born) into *life*, which is the gift of God to the believer. Like Jesus, we also are here not to condemn others but to accept the dismal fact that we are all already under the sentence of condemnation and death, and to embrace the Lord Jesus Christ as our Savior and urge others who are in the same plight (under sentence of death) to do likewise and rescue their immortal souls for life eternal. True, we are all in this together, but what we are all in is not a place of everybody doing the best they can and believing in each other, but the stark reality that none of us can ever do anything of ourselves to break the sentence of death under which all men labor.

What we must all have is a radical change from the old, natural nature to the new, divine nature, and an exchange of the sentence of death to the new life in Christ—a change of position from having been born into this world a child of the devil to the new birth experience by which we become a child of God (John 3). Education, culture, and self-determination will never bring about this change. Neither will riches or fame. The change can be brought about only through repentance of our sins, faith in the redemptive work of Jesus Christ, and acceptance of the Lordship of Christ.

All self-realization religions are humanistic. Any teaching that says man can better himself by his own efforts and thus gain eternal life is humanistic and not Christian. Humanism says man can improve himself. Christianity says man's old nature must be displaced by a new nature, which is a gift to him from God in response to his faith and his acceptance of the kingship of Christ in his life.

Our Father, we thank Thee that, knowing our utter helplessness, Thou hast made full provision for our redemption through the finished work of Christ, whose shed blood atones for our sin. We would not frustrate the grace of God, for if One died for all, then were all dead, and the dead cannot save themselves. We praise Thee for so great salvation—that while we were yet sinners, Christ died for us. We bless Thy name and bow before Thee in humility and gratitude. In Jesus' name, amen.

The "Calvary Position"

The new birth experience is definitely a *miracle*, and it makes no sense to the intellect of a man. The Bible clearly states that this is true. That is why it must be received by *faith*, as a gift from God. It cannot be earned, nor achieved by self-effort, and so it is an affront to man's pride. Man's disposition of vanity causes him to take the position of (to borrow a popular expression) "I want to do it myself, Daddy." Whatever efforts man may make toward his ultimate destiny will end in sending him to hell, whether he goes as a derelict or a philanthropist. Man may get himself to the grave with an honorable reputation, but he will never get himself into heaven. There will be many in hell with honorable reputations. It is not by an honorable reputation that everlasting life is obtained. Everlasting life is obtained, as already stated, through man's recognition and admission of his lost condition and the extended grace of God to him in response to his repentance and faith. There simply is not any other way to obtain the mercy of God. Let the man who plans to get into heaven some other way be reminded that he may gain the whole world (for in a sense, the world belongs to man), but he will not gain heaven; for heaven belongs to God, and He will have the final word.

This is where humanism will have its moment of truth: at the judgment seat. When that day dawns, it will be God who is in control, and man's destiny will be determined by God's laws, not by man's self-righteous idealistic delusions. There will be no tolerance. There will be no rationalizations. There will be no exceptions on the grounds of good intentions. Man will be judged by whether he is found in the Book of Life or the book of death. His protests will not be heard. His achievement records will not be found in that book. Remorse, if he has any, will not help.

This reminds me of the atheist who was quoted as having said to the Bible-believing Christian, "Man, if I believed what you believe, I would never cease, day and night, warning men of their lost condition and need for the Savior." Is it not true? If we know these truths, can we ever be at ease, knowing that the majority of people with whom we come in contact are either willfully or ignorantly plunging to hell? Without a doubt we should be giving far more attention to saving the lost than to simply enjoying the fellowship of those like-minded unless our gathering together includes the ultimate purpose of praying and working toward the salvation of lost souls. For let us not forget that our personal salvation is not the end purpose of God: We are saved with the intention that we will be fruitful, which involves sharing our faith with others and upholding the truth that Christ is the only Savior and the answer to man's need. And if we are to have success in winning others, we shall need the help of the Holy Spirit, for it is the work of the Holy Spirit to convince men of sin and to reveal to a man's inner consciousness the realization that he is indeed hopelessly undone and helplessly lost. This will never happen if we water down the message and substitute a false idealism in place of the truth in order not to offend the sensitivity of the self-righteous. The Word of God is alive and sharper than a two-edged sword and will do a convicting work if it is applied. It is up to us to apply it. And it is also up to us to guard our own spirits from the infiltration of the insidious false teachings that are being perpetrated on all sides by the humanists. Self-righteousness is the archenemy of the Spirit of Christ: It is, in fact, the spirit of antichrist.

If it had been in the power of man to save himself apart from the sacrifice of Christ, then Calvary was the greatest tragedy in human history. If we were all okay, the cross was a mistake. If we are all basically good already, we do not need God. This is the real point of deception in the humanistic view. Man is proud. That is one outstanding trait of his sinfulness. He is so very proud that he does not like to think that he needs God. He prefers to be his own savior because it does not suit his self-esteem to humble himself and admit his need. If all men could admit their need of God, all could be saved. This is the crucial point. The man who will say, "I do not need God; I can save myself," will never know salvation, no matter how much refinement he may achieve. Self-styled morality is not biblical sanctification. Good works are not holiness. Religion is not salvation. Being "good" is not being born again. Ego-originated ecclesiastical activity is only an artificial substitute, not the genuine article. Religious spirits that feed on the natural man's pride are as deadly an influence as evil spirits that plunge men into obvious sin: Indeed, they are more to be feared in that their true nature is often unrecognized.

The humanistic philosophy thrives on man's ego. The seeds of humanistic thinking grow in the soil of self-righteousness, and the Christian needs to be on guard as much as anyone else. Your protection is in the Word of God, not the walls of a church. The foundations of our main denominations were undermined many years ago by a version of humanism called at that time "modernism." This teaching denied the verbal inspiration of the Bible, the virgin birth of Christ, the bodily resurrection, the blood atonement, the physical second coming of Christ, the depravity of man, and the doctrine of eternal punishment in hell. This kind of teaching in our large seminaries and preaching in our mainline churches has spawned a society of churched heathen. We have in America vast multitudes of professing Christians who have retained the respectability of church affiliation but who have a bloodless religion and a humanistic philosophy coupled with a Bible that to them has become only another book, not the inspired Word of God, but a collection of fairy tales in the Old Testament and good literature in the New Testament, and one can take what he likes and leave what he doesn't like and feel no qualm of conscience in whatever he chooses to discard. This was presented to our advanced culture as an improvement over what they termed the old-fashioned "slaughterhouse religion" (referring to the blood atonement). What it became was another "bootstrap religion"—man effecting his own salvation through his own good works and self-righteousness. The theologians sowed to the wind, and we have reaped the whirlwind in the present wide-sweeping surge of humanism.

Man's pride rejects the grace of God because grace is God's favor extended to the undeserving, and man does not want to accept the fact that he is indeed undeserving. His self-glorification demands that God accept him on his own terms, looking upon him as being as virtuous as he sees himself in his own eyes. This is man worshiping man. God will never come to terms with such erroneous thinking. Corrie ten Boom is quoted as saying, "God loves me just as I am; but He loves me too much to let me remain as I am!" The winds of humanism may blow through your television, your daily newspapers, the poets, and even some pulpits, but you will not find this philosophy in the Bible. The hymn writer Edward Mote had it right when he wrote the words:

My hope is built on nothing less
Than Jesus' blood and righteousness;
I dare not trust the sweetest frame,
But wholly lean on Jesus' name.
On Christ the solid Rock I stand,
All other ground is sinking sand.

We need to come back to the *Calvary position*, to maintain a continual spirit of repentance and contrition, to cling to the old rugged cross in conscious awareness that our only hope as vile sinners is the cleansing blood of Jesus, confessing with another songwriter: "I have no other argument, I have no other plea: Jesus died for all mankind, and Jesus died for me." For "there is none other name under heaven given among men, whereby we must be saved" (Acts 4:12).

Infinite Perfection

To look for comfort from the world is to look in vain, for there is neither peace nor solace to be found in any person or any place such as is found in Jesus. In Him all searchings cease and all the hunger of the soul is satisfied. In Him the empty are filled and the poor made rich. He is a song to the sad, a companion to the lonely, and the hope of the desolate. Yes, He is ultimate joy and infinite perfection.

To abide in Him is to rest the soul in a place undisturbed by earthly anxieties.

Gratitude

Godliness with contentment," we are told, "is great gain." Who would not desire "great gain"? It comes through loving God and resting in His provision, whether that be much or little. It does not matter to the contented soul whether it is much or little, for Christ has become the source of satisfaction. (See 1 Timothy 6:6.)

In a world crowded with turmoil and noise, we come into the silence of Thy presence, heavenly Father, to worship Thee and to listen to Thy voice. For in Thy presence is peace and rest. In Thy love is soothing balm to heal every wound and quiet every fear. Omnipotence resides in Thee, and all Thy divine energy waits to lift us out of our weakness into Thy strength. We put away the pettiness of worldly cares to let Thy nearness comfort our souls and the light of Thy countenance bring clarity to our vision. Let us look upon others through the eyes of Thy compassion, and upon ourselves through Thy loving forgiveness, for we are ever in need of Thy mercy. Let Thy benediction rest upon all Thy children everywhere. In Jesus' name, we pray. Amen.

"I Am Ready to Die"

I am ready not to be bound only, but also to die. . .for the name of the Lord Jesus" (Acts 21:13). These were the words of the beloved apostle Paul. They ring out as a challenge to us as to our attitude toward dedication and devotion to Christ. I believe it was Thomas à Kempis who made the remark that we would be wise to think more about how soon we are going to die than about how long we are going to live. Which reminds us of the scripture that says that he who would save his life will lose it, and he who would lose it for Christ's sake will find it.

Life and death is a somber subject. We would prefer to think about health and prosperity. We would rather sing about *living* for Jesus. We may very well be inclined to shy away from thoughts about being bound and dying for Him, but this is by far the greater test of the depth of our commitment to Christ. The Christian life is not all glory and joy. There is a price to be paid, and for some it is greater than for others. Since we don't know how much will be required, it is well to give some consideration to the possibility of the ultimate. You may live in peace and die in peace, rejoicing in the Lord all the way. It would seem that some have, although struggles and sacrifices are not always apparent. In any case, we do well to be prepared to face unfavorable circumstances. It is good mental health to anticipate only good, but the prudent man will also be prepared for the worst.

At this point I would like to diverge slightly from the point and refer again to the incidents in Acts 21. Paul was warned by the disciples through the Spirit (v. 4) not to go to Jerusalem. In 20:22–25, he states that the Holy Spirit has repeatedly witnessed in every city, saying that bonds and afflictions await him. But hear his response in verse 24: "But none of these things move me, neither count I my life dear unto myself, so that I might finish my course with joy, and the ministry, which I have received of the Lord Jesus, to testify the gospel of the grace of God."

Again, in 21:10–12, Paul is warned by the prophet Agabus and by the Holy Ghost that he will be bound by the Jews at Jerusalem. At this point we have Paul's answer: "What mean ye to weep and to break mine heart? For I am ready not to be bound only, but also to die at Jerusalem for the name of the Lord Jesus" (v. 13). Some would tell us that Paul made a mistake in not heeding these words of warning. My personal conviction is that words of prophecy are given to *prepare* God's children for those things they are facing or about to face, rather than to be received as directional. Certainly Paul of all people knew the implications of the prophetic word, and he did not receive it in light of *guidance*, but rather as *preparatory*—and as much so for others as for himself. In the days ahead, when receiving word of Paul's fate, the disciples would no doubt find consolation as they remembered that though the suffering awaiting him had been clearly revealed, he deliberately chose to go through with God, for the sake of the gospel of Jesus Christ.

We can ask ourselves if, being thus informed of the high cost of doing God's will, we would make the same choice as Paul made—to move ahead into the storm, for the same reason: to finish our course with joy, and the ministry we have received of the Lord Jesus, to testify the gospel of the grace of God.

Many there are who have done just this down through the years. We remember David Livingstone, who left his heart buried in Africa for love of those with whom he had shared God's grace. The pages of *Foxe's Book of Martyrs* drip with the blood of those who in like fashion paid the ultimate price for their devotion to Jesus Christ. It was not so much that the martyrs chose to *die*, but rather that they chose to *live* to the full extent of their opportunities to serve Christ, choosing not to retreat in the face of the hazards. It is not a healthy state of mind to desire to die, but it is a very healthy state of soul to be sold out to Christ, to serve Him at any cost, even to death. Indeed, anything less falls short of total commitment, and any love that is limited by convenience and self-preservation is not worthy of Him who gave Himself for us.

We have been thinking about being willing to die for Christ. It is not unthinkable that there may be those who will read this who will be called upon, in one way or another, to do just that. The appalling thing is that so many otherwise seemingly lovely people cannot endure the slightest rebuff with grace. We are all so strongly inclined to be oh-so-touchy, whether the slight offense be real or only imagined. It would seem that we are gravely ill-prepared for any sort of real suffering, for Christ or for any other reason. The pride in us demands to be pleased to the extent that we are resentful of rebuke and ill inclined to any sort of correction. Pride demands only to be approved of. Beloved, this is not the kind of stuff of which martyrs are made. "If thou hast run with the footmen, and they have wearied thee, then how canst thou contend with horses? and if in the land of peace, wherein thou trustedst, they wearied thee, then how wilt thou do in the swelling of Jordan?" (Jeremiah 12:5). If we can't handle an insignificant insult, we needn't waste time fantasizing about singing praise to God while burning at the stake.

It is very revealing and enlightening to read through the Gospel accounts and observe how Jesus handled criticism and insults. And whatever the factors involved in each instance, the significance of His response is multiplied a thousandfold when we take into consideration that He was the Lord of Glory, the only *Perfect One*, and degraded men were thus assaulting Him with totally unfounded accusations. His answers, in some cases, are among the loveliest words in the Bible.

It is time we take inventory of our "grace factor," lest we be found among those who "wearied the Lord with their complaints."

Father, bless we pray all those who are in special need of Thy sustaining strength this day. Be near to those who are in places of danger, and be to them a wall of protection round about. For those in sorrow, we ask Thy comforting Spirit to lift the burden. For the sick, we pray for Thy touch of healing and resurrection life. And for all those who minister to others, wilt Thou, Lord, grant them a measure of strength sufficient for the day. In Jesus' name, amen.

The Spiritual Man

Happy is the man who follows in the footsteps of his Lord. He shall not serve strange masters, neither walk in dark places. The Lord shall be his strength and wisdom, and his heart shall rejoice in the confidence of knowing: God is my judge; He also is my Savior. He shall be upon my right hand, standing beside me, and I shall not fall into the snare of discouragement.

Surely the days shall bring this man joy and happiness, and life shall open to him her treasures. He shall be courageous. He shall do exploits. He shall rejoice that in the day of battle he finds power to stand. His heart shall be at peace because his mind is stayed on God.

Though others be distracted, his eyes are fixed on Jesus, and no turmoil disturbs his inner clam. This peace the world can never give, but it is the possession of the spiritual man, because he has made the Most High, even the everlasting Father, his habitation. He shall not taste defeat!

Heavenly Father, Thy love is to our hearts a consolation beyond all other comfort. Thy presence is peace and Thy voice is sweet. We are privileged to be Thy children, and to have Thy companionship is to experience heaven on earth. Draw us ever closer, we pray, and banish any cloud that would hide from our eyes the clear shining of Thy smile. Grant us deeper understanding of Thyself and of our relationship to Thee, that we may walk in the light of Thy countenance, fearing no evil. Deliver us from all darkness, for Thou art light, and we have been commissioned to shine as lights in the world. Make it so. In Jesus' name, amen.

The Love of God

The love of God is as a sweet song rising above the strident discords of the world about us. We may stifle it at times by our feelings of unworthiness, but still it continues to sing above the storms and penetrate the darkness. All our blindness and bungling cannot silence its pure melody, nor can our deafness banish its beauty. It is there in our moments of awareness as well as in our times of unheeding indifference. God's love is *constant*—unchanged by time, place, or circumstance. Its warmth would melt the coldness of our hearts were it not for the insulating factor of our chosen separation from His nearness. In the light of its flame we would be done with shadows could we but continually bask in His presence. Only our heedlessness can deprive us of the perennial blessedness of the *love of*

God. The distraction of things and the concerns of life take our attention. "In returning and rest shall ye be saved; in quietness and in confidence shall be your strength" (Isaiah 30:15). Why? Because in the quiet place of rest of soul, you will always discover the sweetness of the love of God and hear again the reassuring sound of His voice. It is all around you, above you and within. It is all-engulfing, all-pervasive, persistent, and changeless. Let all else fail: God's love will endure. Count your blessings and put God's love first and last, and if there is nothing to add in between, you are still amply blessed, for His love surpasses all other joys. It is a full symphony of harmony and delight, and the listening heart could forgo all other joys and feel no loss.

The Bible is God's love letter to man, calling him home to the Father. It is God's arms outstretched to welcome the sinner into His forgiving heart. The beauty of nature, the songbird, and the sunset carry the same message. It is God expressing His infinite love. Man can accept or reject. He is free to choose, for it is the nature of love that it is *extended to*—not *forced upon.* The saddest commentary on mankind is that when God's love would most benefit and is most needed to cure an ill, it is often spurned. A crossed will arouses resentment, and the dissatisfaction with circumstances reflects back to God, thus registering hostility toward Him as though He deliberately has interfered with some source of desired satisfaction. The assumption is that God is to blame for whatever misfortune arrives on our doorstep. Falsely we conclude that He may be punishing us for our sin or simply depriving us of joy to satisfy a passing whim or teach us some lesson we are not eager to learn. And so in our moments of discontent, we ascribe to God the kind of character that is foreign to Him, and we lose our inclination to relate to Him in a loving, grateful way. We are not feeling loving and grateful at such times, and it reflects back on God. We are mad—at someone, something, life, the world—whatever— and we are mad at God. In this state of confusion, we go even a step further and presume that He is angry with us, and this relieves us of the guilt of actually being mad at Him. If we were not mad, we would be receiving His love, be saturated with His love, and be sharing His love with others. There would be no grouches. There would be no miserable discontent. There would be no spirit of ingratitude. Whatever our lot, we would praise Him and rejoice; for His love is more than sufficient to flood our lives with joy could we but grasp the wonder of it.

By nature we are carnivorous: We are not easily pleased, and when we are not pleased we take bites out of each other. That is why the Bible says, "If ye bite and devour one another, take heed that ye be not consumed one of another" (Galatians 5:15). A greater measure of the love of God abiding in our hearts would cure this vicious tendency that is all too prevalent, and not (alas) escaped by being religious. (The above scripture was written to believers.) We would do well to ask ourselves why we are angry. A bit of self-examination might bring insight and also might reduce the growing demands upon mental health specialists. The next time you feel down, ask yourself why you are angry. If you don't hear an answer coming back, try forgetting about the fact that you feel disagreeable, and begin to encourage your heart with the remembrance of the hilariously happy fact that God loves you. God *loves you*! Just how angry can you be, or how long can you remain depressed, when you feast your mind on this humongously wonderful truth? It is true that there isn't any such word as "humongously"— and there shouldn't be any such thing as a child of God being habitually ill tempered. It is a disgrace to His grace and a shame to His name. It is time we were done with pettiness, or else we should be more honest with ourselves and stop mouthing so many high-sounding religious verbiages. But for His infinite patience, God would be very discouraged with most of us. Our selfishness is so glaring, our discontent so obvious, our praise so absent, our love so weak. We ought to be sick and tired of being so sick and tired. Why should we take a perfectly beautiful day and spoil it by being spoiled? We cannot pick a rose without cursing the thorn. Unless the hand of death has the power to effect an instantaneous change in our dispositions, we would wreck heaven before we were through the gate. If we could have a bit of the transformation here and now, why not? All cannot be rich and beautiful, but all can be happy, and some of the happiest people in the world are neither rich nor beautiful, and some of the rich and beautiful are most miserable.

There is no price tag on joy, and it often comes by *getting rid of* rather than by *getting*. It is like the water that rushes to fill the hole in the sand on the beach. If we could empty ourselves of our discontent, joy would rush in to fill the space created by discarding the negative emotion. Unforgiveness and resentment are a hedge of thorns that prevents God's love from entering our hearts. Opposites will not occupy the same space. We buy our miseries, for we pay dearly for them by treasuring old grudges.

Heavenly Father, we bring to Thee the love and adoration of our hearts, knowing full well that all the praise we could ever offer to Thee is but a token of that which is Thy due. Thou hast filled our cup to overflowing, and Thy grace toward us has been as the vastness of the sea. "There's a wideness in God's mercy like the wideness of the sea; there's a kindness in His justice, which is more than liberty. There is welcome for the sinner, and more graces for the good; there is mercy with the Savior; there is healing in His blood. For the love of God is broader than the measure of man's mind; and the heart of the Eternal is most wonderfully kind. If our love were but more simple, we should take Him at His word, and our lives would be all sunshine in the sweetness of our Lord." This we pray in Jesus' name. Amen.

The Supremacy of Christ

Heaven is the habitation of happy people, and they are in this blissful state because in heaven there is no unforgiveness. It is not really mosquitoes and briars that make us unhappy: It is festering sores from old wounds that will not heal because we will not forgive. It doesn't matter what injuries we have received. What matters is that we somehow manage to apply the love of Jesus to that old sore spot and let forgiveness heal it up and thus get rid of the pain. Who needs it? If we are not tired of it by now, our friends are tired of hearing about it. Let the Spirit of God cut it out like a surgeon cutting out cancer, and be rid of the deadly disease, for disease is dis-ease, and why preserve the poison?

Submission is another word for love, but we do not like to submit. The sustaining force behind humanism is self-will. We do not welcome interference. This is why marriage is difficult: It infringes upon our independence. This innate dislike for interference is the tension point in any relationship, whether between parents and children, employer and employee, neighbors, or friends. Each relationship spells additional restrictions and fewer freedoms. This is especially true of our relationship with God. He, in fact, desires a *total relinquishing* of our will in order to fully accept His will. At this point, the humanistic struggle ensues. We will either accept His will superimposed upon our own or rebel at His authority and go our own way, thus enthroning self rather than Christ, and in so doing become humanists. Humanism has *many expressions* but a *single root*—self-will in opposition to the supremacy of Christ.

Consider the many who were at odds with Jesus during His life among us on earth. The scene at the cross is conspicuous for the presence of enemies and the absence of friends. Human nature has no time for Jesus and no inclination to be submissive. We are charmed by His charisma but repulsed by His supremacy. We enjoy being *loved and coddled* but recoil at the mere thought of being *loved and controlled*. We can readily admire Jesus as the loving, faithful Friend, but when *submission* enters the picture, we quickly look for an escape. The rich young ruler experienced this sudden change of attitude from admiration to rejection as his will was crossed and his selfish desires violated by the mere suggestion of Jesus that he pay the price to follow by giving up his riches.

To admire Jesus and then opt to continue in self-determined independence is to fail as totally as if the initial attitude were one of hostility. We have given Christ nothing if we offer Him our heart with strings attached. His love for us was expressed by the sacrificing of His life for us. It was total. It is still the same kind of love today: it has no limit, no reservations. It is deep and strong, lofty and sweet. It invites reciprocation of kind but *demands* nothing. We are free to love Him or to crucify Him. The decision is ours, and we make it daily. We make it in a special way at certain crisis points in our lives such as at the time of initial conversion, but we also make it continuously. The Bible tells us it is like the marriage relationship. The ceremony, like the conversion experience, is one point in time, but the nurturing and full flowering of devotion is a process involving years. The submission and the responses of affection are part of a continuing commitment, and any harbored resentment will mar the harmony of the relationship.

Life will not be all joy, but if we trust His love, we will not blame God for the unpleasant experiences in life. I once knew a saintly elderly gentleman who remarked that he had never had any trouble, when in truth, it was a known fact that he had suffered much as an early missionary to China, had lost his beloved wife by the Black Plaque, and had lived many months in a concentration camp as a prisoner of war, with nothing to eat but rice from which he had to separate the bugs. Ah, yes! *"No trouble!"* What a testimony to the love and grace of God in a life to sweeten bitter waters and produce a spirit of meekness and gratitude. This is spiritual maturity. This is refinement of soul, a seasoned spirit, a disposition mellowed through the storms and vicissitudes of life, a vessel shaped into a lovely form and burnished to a deep sheen. No complaint, no bitterness, only the pure, sweet love of God expressed through a character chiseled to perfection by the knife of pain. The secret lies in knowing and trusting the Hand that holds the knife.

*Heavenly Father, we are reminded that there is no greater gift
than the gift of love. It is not always easy to remember this, for
there are so many other issues bidding for our attention. There
are so many things to be done that we are ever in danger of
forgetting that it is more important to be than to do. Save us,
O Lord, from the selfishness that would let our hearts grow cold.
Draw us aside, and in the place of quiet communion with Thee,
renew the fires of devotion and give us tenderness of heart that
we may be more like Jesus, in whose name we pray. Amen.*

Living in Love

Two men were waiting for their flight departures.
There had been several recent crashes with many lives
lost. Remarks were exchanged about the incidents. The
one said, "Well, I guess it's just a case of whenever your
number comes up." The other replied, "Yes, but it happens
that the One who puts up the numbers is my Father!" That
makes the difference as to how we receive the events of
our lives. Knowing that what comes to us is from the hand
of our caring and all-wise Father, and believing that what
He sends to us is sent in love should help us get it all into
focus and see the whole picture in the beauty of divine
providence.

Tears are not always bad: Sometimes they wash the dust
out of our eyes and clarify our vision. Pain is sometimes
more a friend than health. Many a person has found God
in a hospital bed who never gave Him a serious thought

on the golf course. Heartbreak has saved some from the destruction of the pursuit of pleasure. God is not absent when you are hurting. Jesus certainly knew the agony of pain in all its forms—physical, emotional, and spiritual—but without sin, without resentment and the blight of anger.

Whatever else the cup of life may hold, let it be filled above and beyond all else with the *love of God*, and you will come out a winner. Best of all, you will save yourself and others the unnecessary baggage of the whole package of unwelcome, unlovely, undesirable negative reactions.

We all need to be reminded of our blessings every day of our lives and to be urged to consider how greatly we have been favored by the mercy of God. We need to be chided oft for our discontent and our restlessness. Goals are good. They give us incentive to press on; but the present moment is also good, and is to be savored with joy. There is a poem I would like to share. It is not strictly speaking a religious poem, but it has a message related to the enrichment of life through everyday enjoyment of what often passes as commonplace. It is entitled "My Neighbor's Way and Mine," by Nellie Goode.

> *I hurried through life's daily paths,*
> *Some longed-for goal to gain;*
> *The little joys of everyday*
> *All beckoned me in vain.*
> *My neighbor loitered on his way;*
> *I saw with scornful eye*
> *He paused at all the pleasant spots*

I'd passed unheeding by.
Though flowers grew beside the path,
I slackened not my speed;
Friends sought to travel at my side,
I paid them little heed.
My neighbor smile and greeting gave
To all he chanced to meet;
He noted every sunset bright,
And gathered blossoms sweet.

At last with weary feet I reached
The goal of which I'd dreamed,
But to my lonely, joyless heart
Scarce worth the price it seemed.
My neighbor then came romping in,
With song and laughter gay.
I wish I had been wise as he,
And lived along my way.

It is the living in love way, the reaching out to share and care. We are in such a rush. Have you ever tried to imagine Jesus hurrying? He had so little time for ministry, and the world was so full of darkness, sin, and pain; but He moved with measured step and poise of spirit, teaching those who chose to listen and being so human and so considerate and gracious that He followed the greatest sermon ever preached with the biggest picnic anybody ever attended. It has been said, "There is always time for courtesy." May we be delivered from being callous. A pure heart and a warm heart should be one and the same. The Bible tells us that "Jesus went everywhere doing good." That is a simple enough formula. Spiritual gifts are wonderful, but you don't need any special gifts to follow that example other than the gift of love, which is universally available. There are a thousand ways to make someone else's load a little lighter or their life a little brighter. "Now abideth faith, hope, charity [or love], these three; but the greatest of these is charity [love]" (1 Corinthians 13:13).

O Lord, our hearts are filled with joy as we anticipate Thy coming. We would not grow weary in waiting, for we believe the time is very near. Grant that we may be ready, and that as we wait we may be faithful to discharge the responsibilities Thou hast entrusted to us. Speed the light to those still in darkness, and let the blessing of Thy Holy Sprit be poured out upon Thy people. In Jesus' name, amen.

Occupy Till I Come

Be ye also ready: for in such an hour as ye think not the Son of man cometh" (Matthew 24:44).

The truth of the second coming of Christ has been widely preached and much discussed. It has been used to goad lethargic Christians into more active service, at the same time luring others to sit on some mountaintop awaiting His arrival. While it is meant to be the believer's "blessed hope," it has for some been a frightening prospect and, rather than inducing action, has paralyzed with fear.

The closer we come to the return of Christ, the more we need a wholesome, balanced outlook. Neither fear nor fanaticism is healthy. There is a position of peace to be found in every Bible doctrine. There is surely one to be found in the second coming.

Jesus said, "Occupy till I come." "Occupy" is a good, solid, practical word that does not smack of either fear or fanaticism. Neither is it beyond our reach. You can occupy, and I can occupy. The Bible says that He is coming for those who "love His appearing," not for those who fear it. He is coming for those who are "looking for Him," which suggests loving anticipation. Loving, looking, and occupying are all good, wholesome attitudes. The thought of His coming should not be disturbing or unsettling, for whatever produces that state of mind will most certainly make it difficult to "occupy." This word by definition means to employ one's time—to be busy; to take possession of. It is a form of the word "occupation"—being employed—giving attention to business, vocation, or calling. It is unfortunate when the subject of the second coming causes more havoc than joy and when it becomes a distraction from duty.

In everything Jesus is our perfect example. Follow Him through His last two months on earth. Before and after the crucifixion, He moved with the same steady step and with full attention to the thing at hand, whether washing feet or baking fish. No hypertension interfered with His balance in the Spirit. Even on the cross He was free to reach out to the dying thief and to His sorrowing mother, and thus to "occupy"—to take care of the business at hand. His entire ministry was a matter of occupying, of giving Himself totally to His calling; and what was His calling? One description of His calling is found in Luke 4:18–19 (which is a quotation by Jesus of Isaiah 61:1–2): "to preach the gospel to the poor. . .to heal the brokenhearted, to preach deliverance to the captives, and recovering of sight to the blind, to set at liberty them that are bruised, to preach the acceptable year of the Lord."

That was Jesus' calling, and as His followers and

disciples, it is also our calling, and so it becomes our guide as to how we are to "occupy." We are to "be about our Father's business." And part of this is shouldering our own personal responsibilities as morally responsible individuals. It is to care for the Lord's work and to care for your own. It is to keep your house clean as well as your heart. It is to give generously to the Lord and provide properly for your family. It is to be diligent in business as well as to be fervent in serving the Lord. It is not to be caught up in a storm of confusion nor to rationalize that since He is coming soon it would serve best to cancel every venture and sit and wait. No! We are to occupy until. . . !

And that is not all. With every passing day, we see the scriptures being fulfilled in the increase of deception and false teaching and the increase of all sorts of powers of darkness and evil. Of all times in history, this is a time when greater diligence is needed than ever before. It is an hour when it can truly be said, "Darkness covers the earth, and gross darkness the people." It is a time for spiritual warfare and intercessory prayer such as have never been required before. It is a time to be watching, waiting, and fighting the good fight of faith. A time to guard our souls against the spirit of antichrist; a time to make sure we have a supply of oil in our lamps, shoes on our feet, swords in our hands, and the helmet of salvation on our heads.

Never have more winds of false doctrines blown across the land. Never have the elect been in more danger of being deceived. Never has the church been in more need of fortifying her walls with the Truth. Never has it been more crucial that the saints be walking in the light of God's

Word and that they keep themselves unspotted from the world. Yes, Lord, and in the midst of all this, Thou wilt keep him in perfect peace whose mind is stayed upon Thee, because he trusteth in Thee. Martin Luther's grand old hymn "A Mighty Fortress Is Our God" comes to mind. "And though this world, with devils filled, should threaten to undo us, we will not fear, for God hath willed His truth to triumph through us."

Through all the trials and testings that confront the believer, God is our very present help. "When the enemy comes in like a flood, the Spirit of the Lord will rise up a standard against him." The Lord will not desert His children in time of adversity. But there are also responsibilities on our part to be faithful to the path of true dedication. We find in Ephesians 5 the following words of admonition concerning our *walk* as Christians: *Walk in love* (v. 2), *walk in the light* (v. 8), and *walk in wisdom* (v. 15). The total contents of the chapter shed all the light needed to make these points very clear. And following on to verse 27, we have reference once more to the preparation of the body of Christ, the church, for the rapture. And so, while we are "occupying" until He comes, let us also be walking in love, in light, and in wisdom: the love of Christ, the light of His Word, and the wisdom that is from above, imparted to us by the Holy Spirit through prayer and meditation and abiding in Christ. Thus, while we are about our Father's business, He will in turn be working His work of purification and preparation in our hearts and lives.

And the more we walk in the love of Christ, the light of His Word, and the wisdom of the Holy Spirit, the more we will be protected from all the darkness in the world about us and from false doctrine in religion. The Word tells us that we should be wise concerning good and ignorant concerning evil. We do not need to delve into the fine points of cults and isms and heresies. We need only walk in the light of God's Word, and the light will reveal the darkness. The following portions from 1 John 4 remind us that there are two spirits—the spirit of truth and the spirit of error—and that there are two different groups of people—those who are of God and those who are of the world. "Beloved, believe not every spirit, but try [test] the spirits whether they are of God: because many false prophets are gone out into the world. . . . Every spirit that confesseth not that Jesus Christ is come in the flesh is not of God: and this is that spirit of antichrist, whereof ye have heard that it should come; and even now already is it in the world. Ye are of God, little children, and have overcome them: because greater is he that is in you, than he that is in the world. They are of the world: therefore speak they of the world, and the world heareth them. We are of God: he that knoweth God heareth us; he that is not of God heareth not us. Hereby know we the spirit of truth, and the spirit of error" (1 John 4:1, 3–6).

"But if we walk in the light, as he is in the light, we have fellowship one with another, and the blood of Jesus Christ his Son cleanseth us from all sin" (1 John 1:7).

Our blessed heavenly Father, it is by faith we come to Thee because Christ has opened the way to the throne of grace by His atoning death. Through Him we are brought near who were once afar off. Through the shed blood we have received forgiveness and cleansing from our sins. We bless Thee that Thou hast provided so great salvation. We worship Thee from hearts overflowing with gratitude for the grace that reached down to our need and extended to us Thy love; and not only Thy love, but life and health and peace. Grant, O Lord, that those who know Thee not might have the opportunity to hear Thy Word; and grant the needed strength and provision to all those who carry the good tidings of the gospel. In the name of Christ, our Lord, we pray. Amen.

In the Stillness of Worship

In the stillness of worship, I will come to you, My children, and in the hour when you seek My face, I will meet you. For when you come to Me in childlike simplicity, you open the window of your soul to the sunshine of My love. It is not a long way from where you are to where I am: I am close enough to hear your softest whisper and for you to hear Mine! Any distance between us in the Spirit can come only when there are hindrances that need to be dissolved. These may be doubts, fears, unholy thoughts or feelings, or anything out of harmony with holiness and love. But as you place these things by faith at the foot of the cross, they will be washed away by the healing power of the blood of Jesus. You will then find that your communion with Me will be effortless, a natural result of being in harmony; indeed, the atonement means to be at one, so it brings a complete "at-one-ment." It comes by the blood of Jesus: not by tears, not by self-castigation, not by regrets, not by longing—but by receiving forgiveness as it has been provided through the redemptive work of Christ. Forgiveness is not governed by a whim: It is a response to faith. He who, having truly repented, does not "feel" forgiven has failed to appropriate the provision of grace. The law says: You are wrong; you are condemned. Grace says: You are wrong, but you are forgiven. Justice says: You must be punished for your transgressions. Grace says: Christ died for your sins, and you are free from condemnation by faith in Him. Satan has done his worst to destroy you, but Jesus has given His life to save you.

Believe it, accept it, and enter into the joy of the Lord, leaving the shadows behind and dropping the bondages of remorse. Every morning is a new beginning with new hope, new inspiration, and a fresh portion of divine love. Brook no darkness. Walk in the light. *Christ is the Light:* Walk in Him. Let the light of His presence be the light of your heart. No feelings of defeat befit the forgiven. Let His praises be your song and let grace prevail!

Heavenly Father, in Jesus' name, we bow before Thee to praise Thee for every blessing bestowed, every need supplied, every burden lifted, and for sins forgiven through Thy grace and forgiveness. We are ever in need of Thy strength to overcome evil, for it is all about us and within, and we plead the precious blood of Jesus for our cleansing and salvation. For there is no safety in yesterday's victory: We need Thy grace anew for each day as it comes. Deliver us from presumption lest we rest in a place of spiritual ease when the enemy stands at the gate. Keep us alert and watchful, for destruction comes in many forms and often appears as an angel of light. Give to us the brighter light of spiritual discernment, that we may know good from evil and cling to the good. Lead us by Thy Holy Spirit, for Thy glory, we pray. Amen.

He Shall Glorify Me

Jesus, in speaking to His disciples about the promised coming of the Comforter, the Holy Ghost, says this of Him: "He shall glorify me" (John 16:14). He adds, "For he shall receive of mine, and shall shew it unto you." He also adds that the things the Holy Ghost will teach us are the things of the Father that were entrusted to the Son. This is a very important truth: the Holy Spirit has been given to us that we might be taught the things of God the Father and of Jesus the Son. Beloved, we need this. We do well to keep reminding ourselves that our most basic need (after the new birth and the baptism in the Holy Spirit) is the pursuit of the Truth. We need to *understand* the things of God, and to understand, we need to be taught, and it is the work of the Holy Spirit to teach us. The Holy Spirit is the transmitter of Truth, for as the verse tells us, He takes of the things of Christ and shows them to us: He passes on to us the knowledge He has of the things of God. How does He do this? One way He does it is by shedding light on the Holy Scriptures. As we read the Word, trusting the Holy Spirit to illumine our hearts to receive the understanding, He will be faithful to His teaching ministry. It is our responsibility to be faithful on our part to spend time in the Word so that He has the opportunity to fulfill His part in teaching us.

Prayer is the breath of the Spirit, and we must pray to stay alive spiritually; but the Word of God is bread to the soul, and we must also eat to live and to grow. Our spiritual "vital signs" will tell the story as to how well we breathe and how much we eat. We could also talk about the spiritual exercise we need, of walking in the Spirit and witnessing to others, but for the moment we are focusing our attention on the teaching ministry of the Holy Spirit.

Chapter 14 of 1 Corinthians is mainly directed to this subject, for it is the gift and ministry of prophecy that is being discussed. Prophecy has a threefold thrust, as expressed in the third verse: edification, exhortation, and comfort. Or in common words, faith-building, teaching, and comfort or encouragement. And the following verse tells us it is given to minister to others—to the church—to fellow believers. The unknown, heavenly language is for speaking to God (v. 2) and is a sign to unbelievers (v. 22). Verse 14 tells us that the heavenly language is a vehicle for prayer; however, it is limited in that it brings no enlightenment to the understanding—that is, it is not a means of learning. It is by means of prophecy—Holy Ghost teaching—that believers are strengthened and unbelievers come to a place of repentance and worship of God (v. 25).

If believers are to live in victory over the world, the flesh, and the devil, and if the church is going to have an impact on the unsaved to bring them to God, it will be to the degree that there is an underlying knowledge of spiritual truth, which alone can come by Holy Ghost illumination of the Word of God. Emotionalism and zeal alone will not avail. To feel happy is nice but not enough. We hear a lot about the joy of the Lord and freedom (and both are wonderful), but these elements of salvation that feel good must be balanced by a serious search for understanding; for the deeper our grasp of the great Bible doctrines, the firmer will be our faith, the more consistent our walk, and the more steadfast our commitment to the cause of Christ.

And the hallmark of Holy Spirit teaching is that it glorifies not the teacher nor the pupil, but the Lord Jesus Christ. The Holy Spirit always gives the glory to Jesus, and Jesus, in turn, gives the glory to the Father. That is the end of the cycle. There is no provision for our giving glory to ourselves or to each other, and no true Holy Ghost teacher will build the pride of his pupils or seek their admiration. "The Holy Spirit will glorify Me," Jesus said, and by this test you can discern whether or not a teaching is true. All false religions fail this acid test. The idolatrous religions deify their idols, and modernistic Christianity makes a god of their religious activities.

To take it a step further, none of us escape the danger of being caught in the trap of idolatry in one form or another, and this includes born-again, Spirit-filled believers, for idols take many different shapes. It may be the shape of a spectacular spiritual experience, or your pulpit, or my book. It may take the form of your mother or your child. This brings us to the first commandment, which states that we are to love God first and foremost, putting Him above and beyond every other relationship or attachment. This means that we are to love and honor Him more than ourselves, more than our dearest loved ones, more than our spiritual experiences and religious affiliations. It means that we are responsible to Him above all others and all else; and to be responsible carries with it the implication of responding.

Now we are back to *teaching*. If we allow the Holy Spirit to teach us, we become responsible to *respond* to that instruction in terms of *obedience*. Now we come to the crux of the matter. When we see this point, we can readily understand why we would rather hear about prayer than about Holy Ghost teaching. (Our reluctance to accept the responsibility of being taught is also a key to why much of our prayer life is ineffectual; for prayer that issues from any sort of idolatry is not prayer in the Spirit, for prayer in the Spirit is always selfless. We foolishly make demands on God when we pray in selfishness and ignorance. We further imagine that He is obligated to respond.)

When your spiritual ears are opened and you truly hear Holy Ghost teaching, you will immediately recognize that God is laying a responsibility on you to respond to Him, and any idolatry in your nature will come under fire. "You can't serve two masters," Jesus says. "Deny yourself (and everything that is important to you), take up your cross, and follow Me," He says. He leaves no room for a divided heart. Let me hang on to my life. Let me hang on to my friend. Let me hang on to my child. Let me hang on to my money. Let me hang on to my religion. . . . *No!* says Jesus. *Hang on to Me! I'm all you need—always have been and always will be.* Hard? No, it is the way of the idolater that is hard, because a house divided against itself cannot stand.

Webster defines idolatry as "excessive attachment to or veneration for any person or thing, excessive love or reverence for something or someone other than God." Parents may be unwittingly guilty of idolizing their children, husbands and wives of idolizing each other, preachers of idolizing their ministries, and congregations of idolizing their church and their pastor. We are all certainly in danger of loving ourselves beyond proper limits. The Holy Spirit breathing on the Word of God and applying its living truths to our hearts is the only sure remedy for man's inbred tendency to attach his affections to things he can see and touch, and most of all to himself. If honest, most of us would have to confess that we have fashioned for ourselves a golden calf of one form or another; and if we were to be accused of having done so, we probably, like the children of Israel, would defend ourselves by saying that it took shape of itself and walked out of the fire, we being not responsible for its existence.

It is time to stop praying selfish prayers and laying demands on God. It is time to listen to what He has to say to us by His Spirit and through His Word and to start responding in some degree of spiritual maturity to the demands He makes on us. Jesus came into this world to do His Father's will. We have no other good reason for being here. God has no other purpose for our being here. Any other goals we may be pursuing are false goals and will end in disillusionment, not to mention lost rewards in this life and the next.

Loving God more will make you love others better. Worshiping God with your whole heart will make you more loyal to your other responsibilities. It is not that we love Him to the exclusion of all else; it is that we remember and live by the principle that says, *He is Lord. He is first. He is supreme. He is our first love.* To please Him should be our greatest joy; to grieve Him, our sharpest pain. He who has given His life for us has a right to demand that we give no less for Him. He has loved us with an everlasting, all-encompassing, unconditional love. He has loved us in total and complete abandonment, even to laying down His life for us on the cross. We can never even begin to express the depths of gratitude we should feel toward Him in response to what He has done for us. All of eternity will not be long enough to praise, honor, and adore Him who has ransomed and redeemed our souls and has taken us out of darkness and brought us into the light of His holiness, out of the coldness of despair and into the warmth of his unfathomable love.

May our desires be His desires; our highest goal to bring Him joy. May we not rest until we have poured out our lives in sacrificial love. May our greatest delight be to do His will, and to that end, may we give our attention diligently to the Word that we may understand more clearly His divine intention and come more fully to have the mind of Christ (see Romans 12:2).

Blessed art Thou, O Lord, who hast comforted us in all our sorrow and strengthened us in all our distress. Thou hast been our Helper when all else failed, the sure foundation when our feet would have slipped. The help of man is vain; the words of the wicked are empty as the wind. We desire Thy counsel, for only with Thee is wisdom, and Thy words are precious to our hearts. Speak Thy Word afresh, and let us listen with an obedient spirit. Extend Thy grace, we pray, to the struggling souls who plead Thy mercy. Pour Thy healing balm upon the sick; give courage to those who are faltering; bring relief to the oppressed and forgiveness to the penitent. Teach us all to love as Thou hast loved—with joy, with generosity, and with genuine concern for the welfare of others, be they friend, stranger, or enemy. In the name of Jesus, we pray. Amen.

The Unvanquished Force of His Life-Flow

And on the seventh day God ended his work which he had made; and he rested on the seventh day from all his work which he had made" (Genesis 2:2).

God did His creative work and entered into rest. He has been in rest ever since. Furthermore, Hebrews 4:4–11 tells us that God has provided a place of rest for His people and that it is His desire that we enter into it. It is not a place of inaction or stagnation, but of unfolding. We are told that God is the One who is ever-revealing Himself. He can do this without disturbing His rest. He abides in fulfillment. He moves silently in the flow of life. The work has been done. The outflow is never-ending. Having set all things in motion, He quietly observes the outcome.

Yes, and He would also teach us how to enter into rest and how to become observers. For verily His hand is moving, and we accomplish the most in His kingdom when we stand still and behold Him. Educated faith knows that it is not the power to do things for which we need to pray, but the patience to stand still and watch the unvanquished force of His life-flow bring forth the divine purpose. It is not by our striving that lives are transformed. It is by the power of the ever-speaking Word; for His voice has gone out through all the earth.

In like fashion, the Lord Jesus Christ, having accomplished our redemption through His substitutionary death on the cross, cried in His final words, "It is finished." And again in Hebrews 12:2, we read of "Jesus the author and finisher of our faith; who for the joy that was set before him endured the cross, despising the shame, and is set down at the right hand of the throne of God." The work having been finished, He sat down. And we are to "look unto Him." In our daily life as believers and followers of Jesus, we are to draw strength from His finished work and courage from His example. He endured suffering; He paid the price in terms of humiliation and loneliness. He gave Himself freely to the Father's purposes and to the fulfillment of His commitment because of His devotion to the Father and His love for all men. This is the pattern He left us to follow;

but He did more than leave us a pattern. He sent us His Spirit in the person of the Holy Ghost to empower us to give a full measure of love and sacrifice.

The divine intention in bringing us into this world was, and is, that we might glorify Him. The very essence of bringing honor to Him and pleasure to His heart is in our identification with His desires. The more perfectly we relate to His intentions, the deeper our experience of His rest. Conflicts and unrest rise out of cross-purposes. God's abiding place is a place of rest. "Thou wilt keep him in perfect peace [rest], whose mind is stayed on thee" (Isaiah 26:3). To rest in Him is to move in a realm of inner harmony and to be freed from the pressure of self-effort. It is to find the motivating energy of His Holy Spirit moving us quietly through the tangles of life without feeling the need to do battle with the opposition.

To rest in the Lord is to know that He is moving in sovereign authority and there is no cause for alarm. His answer is on the way. His voice is speaking and His hand is outstretched. He who knows the end from the beginning knows exactly where we are and why, and He knows what lies ahead, for He has planned it. To the extent that we enter into His life-flow, we will discover that we have entered into His rest, and we will learn to guard that place from the disturbance of those who have not yet found it.

*Our loving heavenly Father, we pause to praise Thee for Thy
magnificent greatness. Thou art a Rock in this weary land.
Thou art a balm from Gilead for our wounded spirits. Thou art
Jehovah-Jirah, our provider. Thou art a strong tower and our
refuge from the storm. We love Thee, we honor Thee, we worship
Thee, for Thou and Thou alone art worthy to be praised.
Deliver us, O God, from ourselves and the vicious tyranny of
our own self-will. Thou art the King of kings, and we crown
Thee sovereign in our lives. Put our rebellion under Thy feet,
and bend our spirits until we are more nearly conformed to the
image of Thy dear Son, Jesus, who humbled Himself and became
obedient unto death, even the death of the cross. This we pray for
Thy glory, in Jesus' name. Amen.*

The Right to Have No Rights

There is a popular religious teaching abroad today which
by its inherent egocentric thrust becomes a breeding ground
for all the host of self-gratifying spiritual sins (otherwise
identified as pride). It was the beloved author Oswald
Chambers who penned the significant statement "The
only right a Christian has is the right to have no rights."
From this premise, any and all ego-oriented religious
teachings become heretical. If the self-renunciation factor
was only an Oswald Chambers theory, there would be no
valid ground for argument, but the truth he has stated is
merely a striking restatement of numerous Bible texts, not
to mention the fact that it is the thumbnail portrait of the

character of the Lord Jesus Christ. Anyone who claims to be His follower takes upon himself the responsibility to endeavor to live as Jesus lived, and none can contest His spirit of humility. The very fact that He came into this world in the first place bespeaks the truth that He willingly laid aside His *kingship* to become a *servant*. And He is not only a Savior; He truly is our Example.

If the most prosperous and popular preacher in the world promotes the notion that God has nothing better to do than cater to our whims, we do well to raise a question. All his prosperity and popularity and good looks and oratory will never change the immutable Word of God. We each have an individual responsibility to order our lives according to God's laws and His eternal Word, not by some newly hatched religious fad that feeds the ego and pride so basic to our natures. The fact that a seemingly wonderful new teaching is heralded by a handsome preacher is no excuse for blindness. Every teaching ought to be tested by the Word of God, and if we do not know what the Bible says, we had better find out in a hurry.

Every religious teaching will furnish plenty of scriptures to fortify the assumed position taken. It is the scriptures that are *omitted* that reveal the error. For every truth revealed in God's Word, there is a balancing truth that keeps the first in check. Any one truth, like any one virtue, carried to extreme becomes out of focus and dangerous. Overmuch justice without the balancing factor of love can be cruel. Too much love without the balancing factor of justice can be destructive. The rule applies to any virtue or any truth you may mention.

An egocentric message that feeds the selfish, carnal nature has no basis in the Word of God. It violates every principle of redemption. It runs counter to the very nature of the Lord Jesus Christ. Its effect is to spawn religious mongoloids with overgrown heads and otherwise stunted growth. The heads are stuffed with Bible verses and the feet have no strength or inclination to walk the path of the crucified Savior. To fail to present the Christian life as a way of dedication, consecration, and sacrifice is deceptive. To hold before people the prospect that God is some sort of indulgent granddaddy waiting only to grant every wish of His darling children is a travesty.

The Bible warns us that we should be on guard against false doctrine even if it is preached to us by an angel from heaven. In the event that such happens, the thing of vital importance is that we know and cling to the truth. (It is not for us to contend with the false messenger. That is God's business.)

We are told in the Word to "test the spirits." When a question is raised as to a teaching, there are several ways to check. One is, of course, by the scriptures. Another is, as suggested above, by the "spirit" that is projected. If the spirit of a teaching is producing a lofty, arrogant, self-assertive attitude, it is not the spirit of Christ. Pride had no place in the life of Jesus, and any teaching that encourages pride runs diametrically opposite to the entire gospel message.

The gospel message is that one Man laid down His life for us all; and the resultant challenge is that we ought to lay down our lives for others and for Him. Second Corinthians 5:15 reads, "And that he died for all, that they which live should not henceforth live unto themselves, but unto him which died for them, and rose again." The entire chapter bears on the point, but for that matter, so does the entire Bible, so we need not resort to numerous quotations.

To sum it up, if the thrust of our theology is generating a proud spirit, feeding self-interest, and bypassing the self-sacrificing, servant spirit that was so characteristic of Jesus, we are in trouble. We will be judged not by our success but by our sacrifice. It will be not by how many riches we have laid up on earth, but by how much treasure we have laid up in heaven. Not by the beauty of face, but by the depth of grace. It is all too possible to be winners in the eyes of men and losers in the sight of God. The redemption message runs counter to common thought. "You are *in* the world," said Jesus, "but not *of* this world." Beware of a message that purportedly tells you that you can have the best of both! Forget it! Jesus didn't have the best of both. He never indicated that He ever wanted it. Beloved, we shall do well if we gain heaven. Not to worry if we should gain nothing else!

Let it be clearly understood that nothing that has been written is an attack on any individual, for every servant of the Lord is worthy of due respect, and every ministry will be a blessing to many by virtue of the degree of truth that is being preached. This, however, does not in any way relieve us as individuals seeking to walk in the light of full revelation from making it our personal concern to separate truth from error. It is a matter of commitment and responsibility. If every member of a congregation would be faithful in searching the scriptures "to see if these things be true," perhaps some of these lopsided ministries would be corrected or curtailed. In the end, the pew is responsible for the pulpit. We sin in that which we allow. There would be no one to preach to if we refused to listen; but, unfortunately, it is a message that tickles the ears. It is a message as tempting and palatable as a warm donut. Small wonder there is a ready response.

But there is also coming a day of reckoning, a day when every man's work will be tested by fire, and it may not be too distant. Beloved, let us seek God's face. Let us not have worldly riches and poverty of soul. We don't need more when our brothers still have less; and pleasing God lies more in loving than in being loved.

There is no virtue either in poverty or in riches. The Bible tells us of the rich man who died and went to hell and the poor man who died and was carried by the angels into paradise. Fine. Other rich men have died and gone to heaven, and other poor men have died and gone to hell. The Bible also states that it is difficult for a rich man to be saved; but that it is not because of the riches per se, but because of the burden and distraction of the riches. Which is to say, it is not what is in the hand but what is in the heart. If the riches get into the heart, they will weigh down the soul. Poverty can have the same effect. The gospel is not primarily concerned with economics, though that may be a side effect. The gospel is concerned with the relationship of an individual to God, and that is dependent on his acceptance of the Lord Jesus Christ as his Redeemer and Savior from sin.

We have the promise in Philippians 4:19 that "God shall supply all your need according to his riches in glory by Christ Jesus." We have the words in 3 John 2: "Beloved,

I wish above all things that thou mayest prosper and be in health, even as thy soul prospereth." We ought, however, to take note of the fact that the promise in Philippians is preceded by a commendation of the Philippian church for its generosity, which reminds us of the spiritual law: "Give, and it shall be given unto you." And the verse from 3 John 2 implies, it would seem, that physical and financial blessings will come in direct proportion of prosperity of spirit, which should be our first concern.

Religious fads will come and go, but the principles of the kingdom remain unchanged. It is still as true as when Jesus first said it: "Seek ye first the kingdom of God, and his righteousness; and all these things shall be added unto you" (Matthew 6:33). God is watching to see where we place our priorities. He wants to be first. There have been those who preached a so-called social gospel, and we have now those who are proclaiming an economic gospel; but God's Word is still true, and His principles still operate. The communion cup still is a symbol of forgiveness, not finances, in spite of what the most popular preacher may say.

"The soul that on Jesus hath leaned for repose, I will not, I will not desert to its foes; that soul, though all hell should endeavor to shake, I'll never, no, never, no, never forsake!" Praise God, we can trust Him with all that concerns us. "Those who wholly trust Him find Him wholly true." I can stake my soul on God and not be disappointed. He knows my every need. It is my part to love Him wholeheartedly. He will do the rest.

*Our God and our Father, we bless Thy Holy name, for thou
art worthy of our worship. Thou reignest supreme over all the
earth and holdest the universe in Thy hand. We bow before Thee
in submission to Thy will, for Thou art King of kings. Thou
sittest upon the circle of the earth and hast made it Thy footstool.
Grant us always, we pray, an obedient spirit and a fervent
desire to please Thee in all things. In the name of Christ, our
Lord, we pray. Amen.*

We Have Come to Worship Him

Yes, like the wise men, we have come to worship Him.
For He is King of kings and Lord of lords, He is the Savior
of the world, the Light of the world, the Bread of Life, the
Resurrection and the Life. He it is who said of Himself
(quoting Isaiah 61:1–2) that He was anointed by the Holy
Spirit to preach the gospel to the poor, that He was sent
to heal the brokenhearted, to preach deliverance to the
captives and recovering of sight to the blind, to set at liberty
those who are bruised, and to preach the acceptable year of
the Lord (Luke 4:18–19).

And He has done and is still doing all these things.
He came, indeed, to set the captives free. He is still out
to set the captive free; for where the Spirit of the Lord
is, there is liberty. His love and His sacrifice for us frees
us (potentially) from all bondage—to the flesh, to the
devil, and to other men's wills. For when we seek Christ
as Lord and ruler in our hearts, He and He alone occupies

the throne. He is in authority. He is in control. When we give someone else authority over our souls and allow some other person to exercise control over our spirits, we deny the lordship of Christ. He is King of kings and Lord of lords, and He alone is worthy of our worship; we deny Him this place that is rightfully His if we turn to any other to yield our spirits to their domination. This is the meaning of the lordship of Christ: that we give Him our wills and our worship and that we respond in obedience to His commands. It is a basic violation of this relationship if we give this kind of loyalty to anyone else other than directly to Him. This is the heart and the lifeline of the Christian experience. We are not slaves to our own wills, we are not slaves to forces of darkness, and we are not slaves to the will of another person.

Christ sets the captive free! Free to love Him without reservation; free to serve Him without limitations; free to worship Him without compromise; free to respond to the Holy Spirit's guidance within our own hearts. This is the believer's duty before God. It is not his duty to respond to another person: It is His duty to respond to Christ. Christian commitment is a commitment to the supreme authority of the voice and the Word and the commandments of God. "Thou shalt worship the Lord thy God, and Him only shalt thou serve." To serve another is to break the first commandment and thus to break them all. The Bible says that if any man teaches some other message, it is to be rejected, even if it comes by way of an angel from heaven.

There will always be an abundance of false teachers.

They are not our responsibility. It is our responsibility not to respond to the false teacher. The false teacher will put you in bondage to himself rather than to Christ alone. He may start out preaching Christ and desiring God's will for himself and for his people, but somewhere along the way, his own will and his own desires begin to demand gratification and the thrust is turned away from the focal point of serving Christ and Him alone. Satan has many deceptions and many ways to turn truth into falseness. Often the very thing we strive so hard to eradicate becomes the error by which we are overtaken, sometimes without even knowing that it has happened. The devil is very sly. He does not label his tricks so that we may decide whether or not to accept them. He slips in on us when we are least suspecting.

We need constantly to lay our hearts and our spirits open to the sharp sword of the Word and the convicting ministry of the Holy Spirit to be protected against moving off center. We need to find our "in Christ" position and give Him all our worship and adoration and obedience. We need to be constantly reminded. We need to give our hearts to *Christ* and to Him alone—always and forever. We could put it in the words of Elijah: "If Baal be God, worship Baal; but if God be God, worship Him." There is no room in the kingdom for a divided heart. It is not Jesus and the preacher. It is only *Jesus*. Our service to Him must be total. And it must be *by free choice*.

Jesus gave invitations to men to follow him, but He did not *make demands*. He left the following to the free choice of the individual. He did not put a demand on the rich young ruler, and when he turned away, He simply let him go. Watch it when people (in the name of Christ) put demands on you. Jesus did not do that. It is a danger signal. It is a red light flashing that will tell you that self-will is in control and is trying to take control of you. Jesus' call to follow Him is firm but gentle—*and loving*. There is no threat and no warning of evil consequences if you do not "toe the line." Jesus does not threaten with retaliation. He did not retaliate when the rich young ruler turned away. He did not threaten when Judas left the supper table to carry out his plans for betrayal. Sin brings its own punishment of anguish and remorse. We need not punish each other.

Discipleship is following Him—not the preacher, not an overpious husband or wife or mother or anybody else who would attempt to exercise control over our spirits. It is following Jesus—*only* Jesus—now and always. We have denounced the tendency in organized religion to bind people and demand loyalty to structures and personalities more than to the person of Jesus. But let us not be smug. The same error that has befallen much of organized Christianity can overtake us as stealthily as it overtook them if we allow ourselves to go to sleep and leave off watching and praying and seeking the face of God for continual spiritual enlightenment. Be sure of one thing: We are never safe from the designs of the enemy and from the self-deceiving works of the old carnal nature. The old carnal nature is not put to death once and for all when we are saved. It is a daily dying to self-will, selfish desires, selfish ambitions, spiritual pride, and a host of other sins of the spirit. For the sins of the spirit are as real and as deadly as the sins of the flesh. We are not totally and permanently sanctified when we are born again and delivered from such outward things as dope, alcohol, and cigarettes! Those are easy compared to the old demon of pride and the demand of the carnal nature to take control over other people. This was Lucifer's downfall. Nothing has changed. It is as modern a sin as it is ancient—and no less deadly.

God is not pleased. We stand in need of an old-fashioned soul-searching, Holy Ghost revival every day of our lives to keep us on the right track. We need to ask the Holy Spirit to test our own spirits, and we need to test in the Spirit those who stand in leadership. We need to *pray one for another—stay wide awake—keep our spiritual armor on and our sword in hand.* There has never been a more critical hour. *The world is poised for destruction. The devil is mad. He knows his time is short. He's after every one of us, and don't forget it.* We can disappoint him. We can get our hearts right with God and keep them that way by His grace and in His strength—and we can be *victorious!* This is no time to give up, no time for weakness, and no time for a halfhearted witness. We all know what we *should* be doing. We know who we are to be serving and how to serve Him. We need to *do it.* And we need to *help each other.*

Heavenly Father, we lift our hearts to Thee in love and worship. Thou art ever mindful of us and of our needs. Thou knowest our hearts in a way that we do not know ourselves. We pray for the illumination of Thy Holy Spirit to make plain to us the hidden things and reveal to us the secret things that lie within our inmost beings, for we do not have the power to search our own souls. By Thy Spirit try our spirits and bring to light that which is not pleasing in Thy sight. Purge us, we pray, of sin, and take authority over every rebellious thought. Let us be willing to be chastened and disciplined by Thee in order to be brought into conformity to Thy divine nature and ruled by Thy love. In Jesus' name, we pray. Amen.

The Riches of God's Wisdom

How unsearchable are the ways of God, and His thoughts are not as our own. We shall never come to understand His intentions until we seek Him for Himself alone. We will not discover His wisdom by searching in the ways of men. He waits for us in the secret place of communion and meets us in the hour of prayer. He is also everywhere, but to have eyes to see Him everywhere, we must first have a heart to draw near to Him in prayer, for worship is not so much of the intellect as of the heart. God is not so much waiting to be understood as to be loved. It is the posture of reverent adoration that will draw us into more intimate fellowship with the Father, with Jesus, and with the Holy Spirit.

Without the touch of the divine consistently influencing our actions and guiding our thoughts, life becomes a haphazard experiment ending in a maze of confusion and disenchantment. We are not equipped to handle it alone, for man was created as a spiritual being, with the intention that he would maintain communion with God. True communion is more in the will than in the intellect. We shall find God as we seek Him. The scripture says, "As the hart panteth after the water brooks, so panteth my soul after thee, O God" (Psalm 42:1). It does not say, "so panteth my *head* after thee." It is not a "head trip"—it is a heart concern. "Where your treasure is, there will your *heart* be also," said Jesus. The more time we spend in prayer, seeking God's face, the more the Holy Spirit will woo our hearts toward the Lord Jesus, and He in turn will draw us to the Father. A cold heart is a heart that is not being exposed to the presence of God through conscious communion and prayer. Prayerlessness is at the center of most of our spiritual ills. By spending time in private prayer, we can save ourselves many hours of fruitless wanderings. To reach a destination, we do not inquire the way from one who is lost. If we wish to acquire divine wisdom, we are safest to seek it from God Himself. As believers, we are taught by the Word to seek to have the mind of Christ. The orientation of our thought life and our consciousness is to be on things that are above, not on things that are on the earth. Beloved, it will never become so if our lives are prayerless.

Jesus spent many hours in communion with the Father during His earthly life, and even now He continually makes intercession for us in heaven. Prayerlessness is the quickest route to spiritual failure. No eye may see the praying saint, but the outward effects will be plainly visible. The same will be true of the absence of prayer in a life. Nothing is truer than the statement that there are no secrets. The outward evidence is not the purpose of prayer, for we do not pray as the Pharisees "to be seen of men"; however, the influence of prayer in our lives will be felt by others.

We have been conditioned to think of prayer changing things, and this is true; however, the greatest dynamic of prayer is its power to change *us*. And concern about the mechanics of prayer need not hold us back. Many a successful prayer has been prayed by the novice in a crisis moment. We learn in a hurry in a life-threatening situation. It is a cop-out to use the excuse of not knowing how to pray correctly in order to avoid seriously engaging in prayer. God is far more displeased by our not praying at all than He would ever be by a faltering attempt.

There are no reasons for not praying—there are only excuses. If sin is in the way, we need to pray for forgiveness. If doubt is in the way, we need to pray for faith. If unforgiveness is in the way, we need to pray for the grace to forgive. If sloth is hindering, we need to shake ourselves free of the weight of laziness and rescue our souls from its dangers. And if our love for God has grown cold, we need to pray all the more in order to rekindle the fires of devotion, for it was the very lack of prayer that let the fire die.

Heavenly Father, we come to Thee through Christ our Savior, trusting the Holy Spirit to make known to Thee the longing of our hearts, for we do not have the words to express our needs, nor do we know what is best for us. We worship Thee and love Thee and are content to let Thee do with us and in us whatever to Thee seems best, for we could have nothing better than Thy highest will. Grant us grace to rest content in Thy providences. Make us sensitive to the needs of others and ready to respond if You choose to use us as a channel of blessing, whether through prayer or action. Deliver us from selfishness and thoughtlessness. Keep our souls attuned to heaven and our hearts open to hear the cry of human needs about us. Make us ministers of peace and messengers of love. In Jesus' name, we pray. Amen.

Rock of My Soul

O Lord, Thou art my abiding place. Thou art as a covert in the storm. Thou hidest me beneath Thy wings. Thou hast opened Thy very heart and hidden me within! O Thou Rock of my soul; Thou eternal, unmovable, unalterable, impregnable *Rock*! Thou hast lifted my feet from the horrible pit and from the miry clay and hast set them upon the Rock, Christ Jesus. Thou hast established my ways. Thou hast become my firm foundation; yea, Lord, Thou remainest. Though heaven and earth shall be removed and every power be shaken, Thou the Solid Rock shalt remain unchanged. Thou art my eternal salvation: Hide me 'til the storms be passed.

Thou art a mighty Rock within a weary land. Thou hast become my Rock of Shelter. For in the time of trouble I will hide within Thy shadow, and in the day of sorrow Thou shalt be a cool retreat from the burning heat of grief. For Thou driest the bitter tear and makest the inhabitants of the Rock to *sing*! Burdens are lifted: Joy cometh in the morning; yea, in Thee there is no darkness at all. Thou givest the garment of praise for the spirit of heaviness and makest me to rejoice with joy unspeakable and full of glory.

In the day of battle, Thou hast been my high tower: The righteous fleeth into it and is safe. For when the enemy pursueth hot against me, then do I fly to the Rock of Refuge; for lo, Thou art my hiding place, my safety, and my deliverer. When my heart is overwhelmed, I will get me to the Rock that is higher than I. For some trust in horses, and some in chariots, but I will trust in the living God; for thou failest not. Be Thou my *continual* abiding place.

When my soul is athirst, Thou makest me to drink of the spiritual Rock, which rock is Christ Jesus, and hast put within my innermost being *rivers* of living water; yea, never-failing springs of refreshing life. Thou art the source and supply of life abundant and life everlasting. The "new man" is daily supplied with spiritual vitality, as Thou hast said, "The inward man is renewed day by day." Surely Thou satisfiest the longing soul, and the hungry soul is filled with fatness.

Thou givest me also honey out of the Rock. Thy words were sweet unto me, and I did eat them, and Thy words were unto me the joy and rejoicing of mine heart—sweeter to me than honey and the honeycomb; for Thou delightest my soul. Thou satisfiest the deepest cravings of my soul:

Thou art all I need. Thou hast filled my cup: Thou causest my vessel to overflow. O Lord, what need have I of aught beside, and what can my soul desire more than Thee?

For the Rock hath also poured me out rivers of oil so that my joy knoweth no bounds. And when the knowledge of Thee shall cover the earth, the trees shall clap their hands and the hills shall skip; yea, even now Thou hast made my feet like hinds' feet which do skip upon the mountains and run upon the hills. For Thou hast lifted my burden; Thou hast broken my bands; Thou hast loosed every chain. Thou hast put gladness in my heart and given me the oil of joy; therefore my soul doth rejoice in God my salvation. Let it be, O Lord, as the anointing oil upon thy servant Aaron, which ran down even upon his hands and his feet, that my service for Thee might be with gladness, and that the joy of the Lord shall be my continual source of sustenance. Let there be oil in my lamp and oil also in the vessels, that my testimony fail not in the hour of darkness and in the hour of trial.

Surely I come quickly, and My reward is with Me.

Even so, come, Lord Jesus. Let my lamp be burning bright, lest I falter in the night.

Heavenly Father, our hearts are rejoicing in the greatness and wonder of all that Thou art, all Thou hast been to us, and the anticipation of the fullness of Thy grace for this day and all to come. Thou hast never failed: Thy mercies are new every morning. Blessed be Thy name, for Thou art worthy to receive all our praise and worship and adoration. The earth is full of Thy greatness, yet Thou dost touch the most timid soul with Thy tenderness! We bow to give Thee honor, and our only petition is that we may learn to love Thee more perfectly and to reflect that love to all lives we touch. In Jesus' holy name, we pray. Amen.

A Message to Archippus

Archippus is referred to ever so briefly only twice in the Bible, but the few words that are given are very revealing, and they comprise a succinct and quite sufficient biography.

The apostle Paul, in concluding the book of Colossians, writes, "And say to Archippus, Take heed to the ministry which thou hast received in the Lord, that thou fulfil it" (Colossians 4:17). The second brief mention is found in the salutation of the epistle of Philemon, where he is referred to as "Archippus our fellowsoldier."

These few words speak volumes about the character of this man. First of all, he had a ministry in the Lord and was apparently serving with true dedication. Second, to be called a "fellowsoldier" was indeed a compliment. The greatest thing that can happen to a man is that God should apprehend him and give him a special assignment to carry out. The second greatest thing is that he be found faithful in the fulfillment of that responsibility. Everything else for that man is extraneous. God is his goal, and woe be unto him if he should ever halt to seek comfort in anything less.

"Many are called, but few are chosen" (Matthew 22:14). *Many are called to follow Christ—called to salvation—called to the kingdom. . . . Few are chosen.* A man may *decide* whether or not he will follow when he is called; but when a man is *chosen*, there is no alternative. This is a great difference! Archippus was not only called, but *chosen*. His was not the choice. The choice was God's. God does not even stop (it would seem) to inquire as to the individual's preference in the matter. God does not make an apologetic approach to a man to test him first as to whether he would *like* to be chosen. No! He chooses by an act of His sovereign will; and the chosen know full well that they have been not *asked*, but *told*. When this has happened to a man, he will henceforth be totally oblivious to any and all obstacles that may appear in his path. He will go through with God at any cost and will be heedless of what might by others be deemed a *sacrifice*. He is *committed*, but his commitment is the direct result of his knowing that he has been *chosen*.

The "message to Archippus" is a pertinent word to every servant of our Lord who has the call of God on his life. To express it in different words, we could say: Make very sure that nothing takes priority over your commitment to the Lord Jesus Christ and the work He has given you to do. If anything has to take second place, let it be something else. Whatever the demands upon your time or energy, let the doing of the Father's will, as best you understand it, be your primary concern. Better to endure the misunderstanding of friends (or family, if need be) than not to finish the course, not to win the race, and to lose your crown.

Billows of Blessing

There is a river whose streams shall refresh the children of God, and they shall bring joy and rejoicing unto My people, saith the Lord. When My Spirit shall be poured forth, the waters shall flow even to the edges of the wilderness, and all flesh shall know that the Lord Jehovah reigneth, for His glory shall be made manifest unto the heathen—His grace in the midst of His people.

With power and great glory shall He come. His streams shall break forth in dry places, and His power shall come upon the weak. They who have thirsted shall drink to their fill, and they who have languished shall be comforted.

In truth and righteousness have all My words been spoken; for I have power to speak, and I have power to bring it to pass. With resolute purpose have I promised, and to the uttermost shall I fulfill.

When ye call, I will answer; and while ye are yet speaking I will come to thee. Yea, if ye seek Me diligently, I shall pour My Spirit upon thee: Thou shalt be encompassed in billows of blessing.

Our loving heavenly Father, we lift our hearts to Thee in wonder and adoration for Thy gift to us of Thy beloved Son, our Lord Jesus Christ. Coming to us from Thy throne of glory, bringing with Him all Thy love and grace, providing for all mankind the perfect sacrifice for our atonement, we find in Jesus our peace, for He is the Prince of Peace—that elusive element so often difficult to sustain in our own hearts, yet it is always to be found in Jesus, for He is our peace. We need not be in turmoil. Resting in Him and identifying with Him, we have available to us a continuing supply of His grace and love to nourish our souls in divine grace. Teach us, heavenly Father, to more perfectly appropriate divine life, that through us, Thy children, may be manifested to the world about us a greater measure of Thy love. In Jesus' name, amen.

Peace, Goodwill toward Men

Once again the message of the angels rings in our hearts and in our present-day world of stress and discord: Peace on earth, and goodwill toward men. This has ever been the desire of God and His intention toward us, for we were made in His image and likeness, and He resides in a state of unbroken harmony and undisturbed peace. His purposes will not be fulfilled until *His will is goodwill.* His heart is a heart of love, and love will always strive to bring peace. Whenever there is confusion and strife, we can know that God's will is not being done, for His will is goodwill, His ways are perfect, and His paths are peace. The music of heaven is always in tune. If we are ever off key, we are out of the Spirit. If there is a jarring note, it is not of Him. "The wisdom that is from above is first pure, then peaceable, gentle, and easy to be entreated, full of mercy and good fruits, without partiality, and without hypocrisy. And the fruit of righteousness is sown in peace of them that make peace" (James 3:17–18). (For a description of the opposite of strife and confusion, we can read the preceding verses.)

The message of the cross is a message of peace, as we read in Ephesians 2:13–14 that those who are in Christ Jesus have been made nigh by the blood of Christ—for He is our peace. And verse 17, "[He] came and preached peace." Whenever preaching is of such nature that it generates confusion and strife, something is amiss. God will guide our footsteps in the paths of peace. Proverbs 3:17, speaking of the ways of divine wisdom, says, "Her ways are ways of pleasantness, and all her paths are peace." The image of an angry God bent on the destruction of evil is a distortion of His holy character. While it is true that God hates all evil, it is not true that He is a God of hate. He is a God of love and peace. "God is love." It would be a heinous misrepresentation of His character to think of Him otherwise. As has been said so many times, God hates the sin, but He loves the sinner and desires at all times to lift him out of his darkness and bring him into His light, His forgiveness, and His wholeness. Jesus, it is written, came into the world not "to condemn the world; but that the world through him might be saved" (John 3:17). This is the theme of divine grace, the song of the angels, and the music of heaven. Christ came into this world for the express purpose of revealing the heart of God the Father—a heart of love for all His creation. He is not willing that any should perish and willingly made the supreme sacrifice that lost, dying, and sinful man might know once more the warmth of the Father's house and the blessing of His embrace.

"No ear shall hear His coming. But in this world of sin, where meek souls shall receive Him still, the dear Christ enters in."

This is the true joy of Advent: Christ loved us enough to come to our rescue while we were yet in our sins. Came to pour His love out upon us. Came to reconcile us again unto Himself. And so we read in His Word, "He that loveth not knoweth not God; for God is love. In this was manifested the love of God toward us, because that God sent his only begotten Son into the world, that we might live through him. Herein is love, not that we loved God, but that he loved us, and sent his Son to be the propitiation for our sins. Beloved, if God so loved us, we ought also to love one another" (1 John 4:8–11).

Yes, the message of Christmas is a message of peace, and it is a message of love, for you cannot have one without the other. Love will bring peace, and peace will bring love. Beloved, take heart, for there is a day coming when His peace will rule in this earth, even as in heaven, and His love will conquer every enemy. Rejoice! "Now is our salvation nearer than when we believed" (Romans 13:11). Our redemption is near. The Lord is at the door. We look for His soon return. We see the signs of His coming and know that it cannot be far away. What diligence we should show in the use of our time and energies to the fullest advantage in the doing of His will. How we ought to seek to lay aside every weight that would hinder and be daily about the Father's business, putting away those things that are worthless and striving to give ourselves wholly into His hands to love and serve Him unhampered by selfishness. How our hearts should be set ablaze with compassion for others and fortified by His indwelling presence, that all may see "what is the fellowship of the mystery, which from the beginning of the world hath been hid in God, who created all things by Jesus Christ. . . . That he would grant you, according to the riches of his glory, to be strengthened with might by his Spirit in the inner man" (Ephesians 3:9, 16). This quotation is just a fragment from a passage rich with spiritual insight and full of words of encouragement, and which of us does not need a word of encouragement?

Victory is assured, but the battle is still on. We know that He is coming, but until such time as He does come, we are left with the challenge to "occupy" (Luke 19:13). The definition of this word is to "busy oneself," or more literally "trade ye herewith," which I suppose is much the same as to say "be about your Father's business"—don't be idle. Much of the climate in the world about us is casual. A serious concern for doing the will of God may run counter to other influences that bear in upon us. It is the Word of God hidden in our hearts, kept fresh by daily mediation and prayer, that will keep drawing our spirits back into the center of our union with God, sharpen our vision, and revitalize our lives. No half measures will do at this point. This is an hour more than ever before for total commitment to the will of God. And what is His will? We come back to our earlier statement: It is *goodwill*. It is peace and love. Some may say that it is much more (which is true), but however all-encompassing the definition of God's will may be, peace and love will still be at the core of it, for these elements are at the center of ours also, and will be if we are abiding in Him.

May the Spirit of God be poured out upon His people as never before that the world may know that we are His because we have love one for another.

Heavenly Father, in the quietness of this hour, we lift our hearts to Thee, grateful for every blessing Thou hast bestowed. We offer back to Thee in a sacrifice of love all the precious things we have been entrusted. We relinquish all things into Thy hands, especially ourselves, for Thou hast promised to safeguard all we commit unto Thee; therefore we would hold back nothing. The good we give Thee to protect, and the bad we give Thee to resolve. We have not the wisdom nor the strength to keep ourselves. Let us learn with the psalmist to rest in the Lord, wait patiently on Him, trust Him, and commit our way unto Him. Surely He will deliver us from evil and preserve us in the time of testing and trial. With praise and thanksgiving, in Jesus' name, we pray. Amen.

Nothing Shall Be Impossible

The child of God lives and moves in a realm above and beyond the natural senses. His home is God's presence, and his shelter is His wings. His heart is at peace, for he is not relying on the arm of flesh. His mind is girded up with truth, and his heart draws from springs of living water. Surely the Lord is his keeper on his right hand, and his enemies shall be confounded. They shall be put to flight. Because he has trusted in the Lord, he shall be comforted in the day of adversity. He shall be strong in the hour of conflict and courageous in the time of trouble. His ways are ways of peace, and his spirit is tempered by patience. Because he has made the tabernacle of the Lord his habitation, he shall not be brought into confusion. The Lord will lift up his head. He will make his hands strong to war. He shall not fear, for his confidence is in God and his hope is in the Lord. Christ is his salvation and his victory: He shall not be moved, neither shall he be discomfited. Because his mind has been stayed on God, He will keep him in perfect peace. The resources of heaven are at his disposal, and nothing shall be impossible.

Grasp My Hand with Firmer Grip

O Lord God, Thou hast drawn me out of many waters. Thou broughtest me up out of the flood. The billows had gone over me, but Thy strong arm hath brought me through, and Thou hast set me in a safe place. Thou art the keeper of my soul. Thou hast not engineered circumstances to prevent complexity, but at no moment hast Thou been unmindful of my plight. Thou hast brought me through victoriously. Oh, let me not look back; but set my feet squarely upon the road ahead, for surely Thou wilt not fail me.

Thou hast said the path of the just is as a light shining that increaseth in brightness as we move toward the ultimate goal. So grasp my hand, O my God, with a firmer grip. Give to my heart a burning zeal that will not be incompatible with patience, and grant a fresh courage and a quickened step.

Heavenly Father, our hearts are filled with gratitude for all Thy boundless goodness, for Thy mercies that are new every morning, for Thy protection and provisions, for Thy grace and Thy mercy. Had we a thousand tongues to speak Thy praise, it would be still not enough. Grant, we pray, Thy comforting touch to those who grieve, Thy healing power to those in pain, and Thy forgiveness for us all, for we have all sinned and fallen short of Thy best. In Jesus' name, we pray. Amen.

The Children of Promise

Reading in the book of Galatians, we find these beautiful truths: that we are the children of promise, born after the Spirit, born free. This is our heritage in Christ. Praise God! In Christ we are new creatures, and through Him the world is crucified unto us, and we to the world (Galatians 6:14). We are not bound either by the law or by powers at work in society. We are *in Christ*, and as we walk in the Spirit, we have the liberty to please Him who died for us. We are not under the dominion of darkness. We are not slaves to other men's thoughts. We are not captives of the world system. We are programmed not by the daily news but by the Word of God. By His Spirit and through a life of prayer, we can rise above the surging current of the influences that surround us and all the forces of evil. God will not allow us to be victims of circumstance as long as we make it our constant aim to stay our minds upon Him. In Him is all the wisdom and power needed to keep us from the evil of this present world. In Him! We are to "dwell deep," abide in Him, as He in us. This is the secret of peace amid turmoil and love in the face of strife.

Many there are who walk in places of great struggle. Difficulties of seemingly insurmountable magnitude confront many a child of God. But in all these things, we are, through Christ, more than conquerors! Praise His name forever! Let His praises be ever on our lips and His joy in our hearts. No good thing will He withhold from those who walk uprightly.

Yes, we are through Christ children of the promise, freed from the bondage of sin that we might walk in the newness of life and fulfill the law of the Spirit. And we are ordained! Ephesians 2:10: "For we are his workmanship, created in Christ Jesus unto good works, which God hath before ordained that we should walk in them." Letters frequently come to me addressed to "Rev. Frances Roberts." Well, I am not ordained of men, but I am ordained of God: ordained to walk in good works! And so are you. This is why He freed us from the law of sin and death. We are not only to abide in Him, but to bring forth fruit and to "do works meet for repentance." (See Acts 26:20.) Faith and works go hand in hand, for faith apart from work is impotent. James writes, "I will prove to you my faith by my works" (see James 2:18). Any protestation of faith that does not manifest in works is a cloud without water. And the one most cardinal expression is *love*. Faith without works is dead, and works without love are a clanging cymbal. God tests us in the Spirit by the tone of the bell. Love will give the ring of music: Its absence will produce a strident discord.

To walk in the Spirit and to walk in love is not beyond our power, for *what God ordains, He sustains*. God would not ordain the impossible. That would be a denial of His wisdom. In the flesh it is impossible, but, beloved, we are not to be in the flesh but in the Spirit. However, we will never be in the Spirit if we are feeding our souls the husks of the world and its empty amusements. "Our conversation is in heaven" (Philippians 3:20), and we are not to mind earthly things. "For they that are after the flesh do mind the things of the flesh; but they that are after the Spirit the things of the Spirit. For to be carnally minded is death; but to be spiritually minded is life and peace" (Romans 8:5–6). God will sustain us by His Spirit in our quest for holiness and good works, for His Spirit within us is life and power. He is able to work out through us by His Spirit what He has worked in us by His Spirit. His is the enabling; ours is the *choice*. He will not force upon us His righteousness. He has promised to give us the desires of our hearts, and it is His will that we desire His nature. "This is the will of God, even your sanctification" (1 Thessalonians 4:3). Many profess to seek the will of God for their lives. In purest essence, *this* is the will of God for all His children—their purification, which is the meaning of "sanctification." He wants us freed from sin. This is the liberty wherein we are called. It is not freedom to express self-will. Paul, writing in Galatians 5:13–14, says, "For, brethren, ye have been called unto liberty; only use not liberty for an occasion to the flesh, but by love serve one another. For all the law is fulfilled in one word, even in this; Thou shalt love thy neighbour as thyself." It would seem to follow that if we are walking in the Spirit, it would not be difficult to love one another; else why would He expect it of us? And loving one another requires laying aside our personal demands to be pleased. When I was a child, there was a Bible motto hanging on the wall in my bedroom, and it made a lasting impression on my consciousness. It was "Even Christ pleased not himself" (Romans 15:3). Ah, that is the secret! As long as we want to please ourselves, we cannot properly love one another. The two will come to clashing odds in no time. The total relinquishing of our personal rights to be pleased must of necessity preface any true love for God or our fellow man. It is here that all self-realization philosophies reveal their counterfeit nature. I do not need to waste time studying pseudo religions to know myself. I can accept God's indisputable verdict that I am a hopeless, helpless sinner, the same as every other human being born into the world. That lets us know precisely where we are starting from: in total need of spiritual transformation, not religious education. The transforming power is there for those who choose to become children of the promise through faith in the finished work of the Lord Jesus Christ and His cleansing blood.

We live in an increasingly permissive society where individuals are encouraged to think and do as they please regardless of moral and spiritual responsibility to God. We are inundated with religious teachings that would have us believe that Jesus, if He ever lived at all, was only one of many good men. To believe in any number of holy men still leaves us without a *Savior*. Jesus was infinitely more than a good and holy man. He is conspicuously unique in His birth, death, and resurrection. There may be many teachers, but only *One* laid down His life as the Lamb of God, slain for our sins and for our salvation. False religions conveniently ignore this by teaching that we are all good and do not need regeneration. They say you are good and can become better. The Bible says you are *dead* and need to be born again to have *life*. There is not a *comparison* between Christianity and other religions: There is only *contrast*!

Praise God if His truth has reached your heart and His Spirit has brought you life. It is not by works, lest we boast. It is by His sovereign mercy that He has saved us and washed us in His blood and made us new creatures. Rejoice! And do not let the winds of false doctrine blow your barque off course. Share the Light, share His love, and walk in the liberty whereby He has made us free, not being entangled again with the yoke of bondage.

Heavenly Father, look down upon us in Thy mercy; blot out our transgressions, and forgive our sins. When we ought to be full, we are empty, and we are weak when we should be strong. We are not deserving of Thy favor, for we have missed the mark and tried Thy patience. Grant us a spirit of repentance. A broken and contrite heart, Thou wilt not despise. If it were not for Thy mercy, we would all be consumed. Lift us, O Lord, out of the place of destruction. Wash us from our sins, and cleanse us of our iniquities. Make this day a new beginning as we trust for Thy redeeming power to operate in our lives. In Jesus' name, amen.

The Voice of the Beloved

I will lift up mine eyes unto the hills. . . . My help cometh from the LORD" (Psalm 121:1–2). Surely the Lord will undertake for all those who put their trust in Him. He is a very present help in time of need. He is a buttress and a fortress, a strong tower and a refuge in the time of storm. His children will never be forsaken, and His eye is ever upon them to do them good. Let us encourage our hearts in the Lord, and let us praise Him in all things, for His goodness endures forever and His mercies greet us with every new day. Praise is comely, and it is good to sing praises unto God.

Such should be our daily frame of mind, and in such a state, the incessant annoyances of life can more easily be relegated to the insignificant place they deserve. Unless my memory fails me, there is a story told about Eli Whitney, who it is said had a marvelous faculty of concentration, and a lovely shock of white hair. His companions, being somewhat irritated by the fact that nothing seemed to have the power to distract him, emptied an inkwell on his head. Their malicious act was still met with composure and disregard. What a victory we could gain over the devices of the enemy of our souls to distress us if we could have as firm a concentration on God as Eli Whitney had on his work!

God should be ever the center of our attention, and since everything about Him is of the nature of encouragement, we would be always well on our way to a peaceful, happy state of mind and a strong, courageous spirit.

We live, unfortunately, in a very egocentric society. We are constantly confronted with an endless variety of things that draw our attention to ourselves and to one another. We are personality-conscious. It requires, therefore, some concentrated effort to direct our focus toward God rather than man. Until we are able to do this, we will always be spiritually out of balance in proportion to the distraction.

In order to worship God in Spirit and in truth—genuinely and in simplicity—the mind must be cut free from selfish concerns and worldly thoughts. This cannot be achieved in a fleeting moment. It takes not only desire and discipline, but *time*—much time in order to wash out intruding thoughts and pull the *mind* into the sanctuary of *worship*. And it takes *more time* in the attitude of worship to draw the *heart* into a state of *devotion*. To declare our love for God is only the beginning. It is in time spent in prayer that the fire of holy love is kindled in our souls. We come to love God by spending time in His presence. It is exposure to Him that deepens our love. Education in theology will not do it. Ritual will not do it. God will do it Himself within us as we seek His face and as His Holy Spirit within our hearts communes in prayer with God the Father and with Jesus, our Lord.

When this chain of communion begins to operate and the Spirit within us is fellowshipping with God the Father, through Jesus, our great High Priest, the transforming power of God moves in and through the human vessel doing a purifying work beyond our comprehension. Old things begin to pass away, and all things become new. Shadows are dispelled and darkness is dispersed by the light. Stubborn bones are broken, and the will begins to yield to conform to the image of Christ. Things that used to matter are no longer important, and doing the will of God becomes a consuming passion. Chaff is blown away by the wind of the Spirit. His voice becomes as beautiful music to our ears, and any contrary voice is an immediate strident discord. This is how His sheep hear and recognize His voice and will not follow the voice of a stranger.

Have you prayed for discernment? Spend more time in His presence in worship, and listen to His voice. When you know the sound of His voice, you will never be fooled by the hireling. Such protection against deception is in itself a valuable reward for time spent in prayer. But if an hour, or a half hour, seems to be a burden, it is only so if you have not heard His voice. When you hear His voice, prayer will become the supreme joy of your life and you will begrudge time spent in any other pursuit. When He speaks, a hundred horses could not drag you from your knees. The keenest imagination could never conceive of a more magnificent obsession.

Whether you have a broken heart or a broken leg, whether you are in a place of despondency or in need of guidance, whether overburdened or overbored, time spent in fellowship with the heavenly Father in prayer will bring a radical change in outlook. It will wash the soul and the mind of clutter as the waves bathe the seashore. It will lift the burden and let the sun break through the clouds. It will bring clarity of vision and a lightness of heart surpassing any other avenue of sought-for relief. There is an old song that says, "I used to tell my neighbors, but now I tell the Lord." How much better—both for you and for the neighbors! The neighbors have their own share of problems. Jesus is the burden-bearer. He is presented in this light particularly in the Gospel of Mark. He has invited us to cast our burdens upon Him, for His concern is for us. We can cast them moment by moment in an act of faith, but we can cast them most completely in times of concentrated prayer and worship when we deliberately and forcibly put every other activity and every other person out of our consciousness and center upon the presence and the person of God Himself.

Difficult? Yes, it is difficult, but as with everything, we have to start somewhere. If first attempts seem to fail, we must not despair. It is within reach of every soul to get through to God. God is always available. It is only our own state of mind that hinders. God dwells in the secret, silent place. We must therefore come alone and in quietness. But, alas, we are not accustomed to being quiet, and we are all too seldom truly alone. Why do you suppose Jesus spent long nights out in the mountains? He was creating for His own soul a place of solitude and peace. It bears repeating: "The world is too much with us." We are too encumbered with things and people—with our own selves, our own thoughts, our fears, our hopes, our ambitions, and our frustrations.

God did not ask us to pray in order to lay upon us still one more burden: He invited us to find through prayer the one most perfect solution to our anxieties and stress, to our sorrows and loneliness. He is the One who so genuinely cares and so totally meets our needs. To put off praying until we solve our problems is like waiting until after the rain to put up the umbrella. The more pressed we are for time, the more essential it is that we give God the choicest hours of the day. The greater the demands of other people on our energies, the more critical our need for precious time alone with Him. We are not considering *options*, because it is not a matter of choosing between prayer and something else. There is no substitute and no alternative.

Prayer is as vital to the spiritual life of the believer as air is to his physical life. Worship is of such supreme importance that it is in essence the heart of the first commandment. This calls to mind the word: "Where your treasure is, there will your heart be also." The more God becomes to us our dearest treasure, the more our hearts will be drawn toward Him in devotion and fellowship; and the more time we spend in devotion and fellowship, the more truly He will become our dearest treasure.

What pursuit could be more fulfilling? This is a treasure not corroded by time nor tarnished by decay. This is a treasure that will not be left behind when we leave this world. This is a treasure that will enhance this life and the life to come. This is eternal, changeless, ever unfolding, ever growing more precious in both time and eternity. Is it not worthy of the greatest investment we can possibly make each day of our lives? Kings die and leave behind their crown and jewels. Architects die and leave behind their magnificent buildings. Scientists die and leave behind their brilliant discoveries. The Christian dies, and his most precious treasure, the Lord Jesus Christ, God the Father, and all the riches of heaven are waiting for him on the other side!

What a heritage we have! What a privilege to be children of the King of kings! What a joy to be heirs of salvation! What an unspeakable blessing that we unworthy mortals can walk each day hand in hand with the Lord of glory! How happy we should be—how grateful! May our ears catch the strains of heaven's celestial music and our feet be like those of the hinds that skip upon the hills. Let our lips be filled with praise and our mouths proclaim His salvation, for He is worthy. He is the Rose of Sharon, the Lily of the Valley, the Bright and Morning Star. His voice is "as the sound of many waters" (Revelation 1:15). "Thou that dwellest in the gardens, the companions hearken to thy voice: cause me to hear it" (Song of Solomon 8:13).

No considerations concerning prayer are complete without mention of the Word of God as contained in the Bible. Many years ago I captured a quotation from Dr. Harry Ironside and wrote it in the front of my Bible:

"Prayer without the Word may lead to fanaticism and heathenism. The Word without prayer may lead to coldness of heart." The two should never be divorced. Prayer and the Word: the Word and prayer. Never neglect one in preference for the other. If you desire to hear His voice, you will never hear it more clearly than through His written Word, especially as the Word is quickened to your heart by the Holy Spirit. Every reading of the Word should be prefaced by prayer for the illumination of the Holy Spirit on the sacred page. All scripture was given by inspiration to holy men who were moved upon by the Holy Spirit. Can we then find a better teacher than the Holy Ghost?

Something to Think About

God listens to our thoughts and conversations. Malachi 3:16 tells us, "They that feared the LORD spake often one to another: and the LORD hearkened and heard it, and a book of remembrance was written before him for them that feared the LORD, and that thought upon his name." And the following verses read, "And they shall be mine, saith the LORD of hosts, in that day when I make up my jewels; and I will spare them, as a man spareth his own son that serveth him. Then shall ye return, and discern between the righteous and the wicked, between him that serveth God and him that serveth him not" (vv. 17–18).

It is both comforting and sobering to know that God is an unseen witness to all our thoughts and conversations. To be always mindful that it is true would be a constant safeguard against unworthy and unholy words and thoughts. Let us determine that He shall hear from our lips only things that would honor Him!

I Kept Them in My Heart

But Mary kept all these things, and pondered them in her heart.
LUKE 2:19

Yes, I kept them in my heart,
The moments mothers treasure;
The gentle words, the thoughtful deeds,
The hours shared in pleasure.
The walks across the fields
With fragile lilies strewn,
The tasty lunch upon the hill
When skies were bright at noon.

Those precious days of happiness
Ere yet He was a man,
Before the days of suffering
And sacrifice began. . .
I loved Him much, I loved Him well,
For He was as no other:
Who else would say upon a cross,
"Friend, will you care for Mother?"

I gave Him all I had to give
Of understanding love;
He gave me from His richest store,
For He was from above.
My son—but deep within my heart

And burning like a fire
I knew, whatever others said,
His destiny was higher.

I kept the words of Gabriel
More sacred than all other:
Yes, I would have a baby boy,
But *God* would be His Father!
We shared the joy, we shared the woe
That are of life a part,
But as he died upon the cross
A sword passed through my heart.

The darkest day in history
For all mankind, 'tis true,
But who can bear the loss of one
Who is a part of you?
Had He not told me many times
He would return again,
I would have died beneath that cross
In anguish and in pain.

Three days and nights in darkness
No human words can tell;
We waited while He grappled
With Satan, death, and hell.
And on that resurrection morn
When heaven with anthems thrilled,

My joy exceeded all my griefs
And all the storm was stilled.

Whatever lies ahead for me
I know that I can bear it,
For now, abiding in my heart
I have His Holy Spirit.
And greater miracle than all,
Believe me, it is true,
Receive His Holy Spirit, friend,
Christ will be born in *you!*